To Our Readers:

Dedication

*To each other and to
that entity with a life of its own:
our relationship.*

T·H·E AFFIRMATIONS BOOK FOR SHARING

An Advanced Program For Building Your Relationship One Day At A Time

Randy & Jay Rolfe

Health Communications, Inc.
Deerfield Beach, Florida

Publisher: Health Communications, Inc.
          3201 S.W. 15th Street
          Deerfield Beach, FL 33442-8190

Cover design by Barbara Bergman

Introduction

The Affirmations Book For Sharing is the first book designed exclusively for a couple to read back and forth. We hope it will become a staple for nurturing relationships, whether you're newly engaged, celebrating a seventh or seventeenth anniversary, planning a wedding, or simply taking a positive step toward a happier life together. Even if you're not part of a couple, these pages can help enrich your present and future relationships.

In writing this book, we drew on the many challenges and successes of our experiences together — through '60's campus courtship, urban professional life, rural homesteading, and now home-based enterprises and a life we share with our two children.

As we approached our twentieth anniversary a few years ago, we had each discovered the value of personal affirmations. Sometimes we read to each other one we especially liked. Soon we noticed benefits far out of proportion to the small effort we spent.

We wished for a book of special affirmations expressly designed to read back and forth.

Over the following year, we wrote *The Affirmations Book For Sharing*. To our personal experience, we added Randy's insights from over a decade as a human relations trainer, therapist, writer and self-help facilitator.

v

We're gratified the many couples who have tried our book share our excitement over it.

How To Use This Book

Each day begins with a few thoughts on sexual intimacy, finance, friends, job, stress, anger, boundaries or another crucial area of our shared lives.

Then follow with two series of affirmations, one to read to yourself and one to read aloud with your partner. The personal affirmations prepare you to get the most out of sharing the reciprocal affirmations.

In each series you have the chance to affirm yourself and your partner by using "I," "we," "you," "she" or "he," and "they" statements.

The positive echoes of these different voices can overcome old negative messages that can interfere with your present efforts to build your love and trust.

The reciprocal affirmations are the core of the book and give you the direct experience of building your relationship together, one day at a time.

After you have read them to your partner, you may find the most profound effects of all come from hearing your partner read them to you.

Benefits

Learning experts say the most effective way to absorb a new idea is to experience it three ways: to read it, say it and hear it. It's impossible to list all the benefits you can get from *The Affirmations Book For Sharing*. We are still discovering new ones. We urge you to begin now to discover them yourselves.

- Set aside a few minutes each day for *The Affirmations Book For Sharing*, preferably in the morning.

vi

- Read the reading and all the affirmations to yourself before sharing the reciprocal affirmations. (We've found it helpful to each have our own personal copy of the book.)
- Maintain eye contact as much as possible.
- Decide together on some system for deciding who will go first or any other procedural points that might cause you to tense up.
- Don't comment on the way your partner participates in the process.
- If you want to discuss a topic raised by a reading, then decide on a time limit, discuss it without criticism, condemnation or complaint and agree that it is all right to disagree.
- Don't worry if an affirmation does not strike you as true right now. If you can imagine it or wish it were true, go ahead.
- If an affirmation is too uncomfortable for you, feel free to decline to use it without any explanation — and accept your partner's right to do the same.
- If your partner isn't interested now, avoid insisting and set a date to ask again; then just go ahead yourself. Your growth encourages your partner to join later. And if their enthusiasm doesn't match your own, don't worry. Stick with it. It will work.
- Don't try to force your partner to follow these tips.

A Few Details

What's In A Name?

The affirmations call for the frequent use of your name. You'll quickly catch on to filling them in as you go. Hearing your names associated with completely positive statements is the quickest way we know of to empower and renew ourselves.

Vive la/le Difference

We have made as few assumptions as possible about sex roles. As far as we can determine, the only predictable difference between any particular woman and any particular man is that the woman has the physical organs to conceive, carry and suckle an infant, and the man has the physical organs to impregnate a woman.

Assumptions about sex roles are a major source of tension and the sooner we drop them the better. Your natural sexuality manifests most easily when you each recognize in the other the freedom to be uniquely yourselves.

Sex-Linked Language

We have chosen the form she/he and her/him for those times when the general "they" didn't work. We wish our language had a more satisfactory way of handling this issue, but meanwhile we've tried to minimize any inconvenience.

If this book helps you enrich your lives together and gain a sense of mastery over the health and joy of your relationships, we will have accomplished our goals.

Randy and Jay Rolfe

We can start our relationship fresh with each new encounter. We aren't limited by our past patterns even if the other person seems to be playing by old rules. Each day we are free to make new decisions, react in new ways and develop new responses.

As a new year begins, we can refresh our relationship by letting go of habitual words and actions that didn't work for us and trusting ourselves to find new words and actions that leave us feeling good about ourselves.

We can forgive ourselves our past burdens or imperfections and build on our past successes. These successes give us direction as we start out across the clean slate of this new year and this first day.

Personal Affirmations

Today I, (your name), begin my relationships anew.

Today you, (your name), begin your relationships anew.

Today (your name) begins her/his relationships anew.

Today we, (your name) and (other's name), begin our relationships anew.

Reciprocal Affirmations

Today I, (your name), begin our relationship anew.

Today you, (other's name), begin our relationship anew.

Today we, (your name) and (other's name), begin our relationship anew.

Today (your name) and (other's name) begin their relationship anew.

Sometimes we adopt goals we get from outside ourselves, goals we think we should want. Parents, school, employer or other authority may have given us goals we cling to. We may feel we've failed because we haven't accomplished these goals, when in fact they were never really our goals. We may have avoided having any goals at all to prevent that feeling of failure.

Now we can affirm our freedom to choose goals that are right for us and to change them as we choose. There are no "shoulds" in whom we choose to be close to or what we get from other people in our lives. We can decide what we want and set goals accordingly.

Personal Affirmations
I, (your name), choose goals that reflect what I want most in my relationships.
You, (your name), choose goals that reflect what you want most in your relationships.
(Your name) chooses goals that reflect what she/he wants most in her/his relationships.
We, (your name) and (other's name), choose goals that reflect what we want most in our relationships.

Reciprocal Affirmations
I, (your name), choose goals that reflect what I want most in our relationship.
You, (other's name), choose goals that reflect what you want most in our relationship.
We, (your name) and (other's name), choose goals that reflect what we want most in our relationship.
(Your name) and (other's name) choose goals that reflect what they want most in their relationship.

We all make plans, both individually and with others. Many times our plans change. Maybe we changed our plans when an opportunity we liked better came up. Or an earlier activity took longer than we expected. Perhaps we didn't consult others whose cooperation we needed or another person involved had a change.

It's okay to change plans. While it's important not to be indecisive, continually change goals or always do what someone else wants, changes in plans aren't cause for upset. Both we and other people have freedom to change our plans.

Personal Affirmations

I, (your name), accept that it's all right for plans to change.

You, (your name), accept that it's all right for plans to change.

(Your name) accepts that it's all right for plans to change.

We, (your name) and (other's name), accept that it's all right for plans to change.

Reciprocal Affirmations

I, (your name), accept that it's all right for our plans to change.

You, (other's name), accept that it's all right for our plans to change.

We, (your name) and (other's name), accept that it's all right for our plans to change.

(Your name) and (other's name) accept that it's all right for their plans to change.

I enjoy interacting with people who meet my needs. Some of my needs are touching, intimacy, support, praise, empathy, personal space, relaxation and fun. I can meet these needs from a variety of relationships.

If I have relationships that are negative, destructive or just don't meet my needs, I no longer have to continue them. I deserve to have relationships that meet my needs. I feel good enough about myself to make changes so my relationships meet my needs.

Personal Affirmations

I, (your name), let go of relationships that don't meet my needs.

You, (your name), let go of relationships that don't meet your needs.

(Your name) lets go of relationships that don't meet her/his needs.

We, (your name) and (other's name), let go of relationships that don't meet our needs.

Reciprocal Affirmations

I, (your name), let go of relationships that don't meet my needs.

You, (other's name), let go of relationships that don't meet your needs.

We, (your name) and (other's name), let go of relationships that don't meet our needs.

(Your name) and (other's name) let go of relationships that don't meet their needs.

So often in our daily activities we feel we should be working faster, focusing on something else or putting off others' or our own pleasure until more is accomplished.

But we owe it to ourselves to give our focused attention to our relationships from time to time. We can accept emotional support and new energy from people close to us to facilitate our other activities. We can feel valuable and important just by giving a moment of emotional support to others.

Intimacy is built one moment at a time. It requires our full attention. We deserve to enjoy the benefits of giving our attention, free of distraction and preoccupation.

Personal Affirmations

I, (your name), take time to enjoy intimate moments with those close to me.

You, (your name), take time to enjoy intimate moments with those close to you.

(Your name) takes time to enjoy intimate moments with those close to her/him.

We, (your name) and (other's name), take time to enjoy intimate moments with those close to us.

Reciprocal Affirmations

I, (your name), take time to enjoy intimate moments with you.

You, (other's name), take time to enjoy intimate moments with me.

We, (your name) and (other's name), take time to enjoy intimate moments together.

(Your name) and (other's name) take time to enjoy intimate moments together.

We tend to have expectations of others close to us. The closer they are, the stronger and more numerous our expectations may be. Sometimes our expectations reflect behaviors we as children either took for granted or longed for, like attentiveness, protection or communication. Sometimes our love fades because we expect the other to be perfect or to meet a romantic ideal.

We don't have the right or power to insist another meet our expectations. We must look to ourselves to satisfy our needs and allow others to be true to themselves as best they can. Love flourishes when we enjoy the perfection we see, rather than the one we dream of.

Personal Affirmations

I, (your name), expect only that others be true to themselves.

You, (your name), expect only that others be true to themselves.

(Your name) expects only that others be true to themselves.

We, (your name) and (other's name), expect only that others be true to themselves.

Reciprocal Affirmations

I, (your name), expect only that you be true to yourself.

You, (other's name), expect only that I be true to myself.

We, (your name) and (other's name), expect only to be true to ourselves.

(Your name) and (other's name) expect only to be true to themselves.

When we're creating a new relationship, we may mistake a new habit for a commitment. We may spend time together, live together and act as if we are a pair without making a commitment to the relationship. We may cultivate a habit of being together, relying on each other, telling each other what's going on in our lives. But we need a commitment of our personal energy to make a relationship work for the long term. We need a commitment that, if comfortable habits are jarred by growth and change, we will be willing to adjust, grow and change ourselves. We need a commitment of personal faith that things will work out if we work at them.

Personal Affirmations

I, (your name), commit myself to working at my relationships.

You, (your name), commit yourself to working at your relationships.

(Your name) commits herself/himself to working at her/his relationships.

We, (your name) and (other's name), commit ourselves to working at our relationships.

Reciprocal Affirmations

I, (your name), commit myself to working at our relationship.

You, (other's name), commit yourself to working at our relationship.

We, (your name) and (other's name), commit ourselves to working at our relationship.

(Your name) and (other's name) commit themselves to working at their relationship.

In a close relationship we may feel we can read each other's minds. We develop our own shorthand for communication and we think we know what the other wants. But for our relationships to grow, we must each be free to grow and change. Otherwise our expectations of the other become oppressive over time.

If we second-guess or assume we know our loved one's thoughts, we may be surprised. We may discover we are doing things for no reason, when we think we know what they want. We bring distress on ourselves — when all we really need to do is ask.

Personal Affirmations

I, (your name), recognize others' freedom of thought.

You, (your name), recognize others' freedom of thought.

(Your name) recognizes others' freedom of thought.

We, (your name) and (other's name), recognize others' freedom of thought.

Reciprocal Affirmations

I, (your name), recognize your freedom of thought.

You, (other's name), recognize my freedom of thought.

We, (your name) and (other's name), recognize each other's freedom of thought.

(Your name) and (other's name) recognize each other's freedom of thought.

Many of the disagreements and tensions we have with our loved ones originate in our own concerns and preoccupations. We are so busy working, accomplishing and doing that we put off feeling our feelings, cutting our worries down to size or keeping things in perspective. Then, if someone crosses us unexpectedly, our negative emotional energy lights on them. We blow a small misunderstanding out of proportion. We add a new injury to our list of old ones.

Today I will acknowledge my problems and concerns and own them myself. I will not attribute my uneasiness to others. I will see and hear the best in others and will deal on my own time with my preoccupations.

Personal Affirmations

I, (your name), own my own worries.

You, (your name), own your own worries.

(Your name) owns her/his own worries.

We, (your name) and (other's name), each own our own worries.

Reciprocal Affirmations

I, (your name), own my own worries.

You, (other's name), own your own worries.

We, (your name) and (other's name), each own our own worries.

(Your name) and (other's name) each own their own worries.

Tension in a relationship comes more often from flareups of temper over little things than from major differences. If we take offense easily and magnify a hurt with thoughts like, "How could you?" or "You should know better," or "Who do you think you are?" we easily escalate a spark into an explosion.

Instead of blaming each other for starting it or escalating it, we need to accept the likelihood of misunderstandings or occasional provocations and make a commitment together to recognize them, identify them, inject some humor or just walk away from them with a minimum of rancor. This shared commitment will help to cool sensitive tempers.

Personal Affirmations

I, (your name), stay cool to avoid occasional provocations.

You, (your name), stay cool to avoid occasional provocations.

(Your name) stays cool to avoid occasional provocations.

We, (your name) and (other's name), stay cool to avoid occasional provocations.

Reciprocal Affirmations

I, (your name), stay cool to avoid occasional provocations.

You, (other's name), stay cool to avoid occasional provocations.

We, (your name) and (other's name), stay cool to avoid occasional provocations.

(Your name) and (other's name) stay cool to avoid occasional provocations.

An important part of any relationship is helping the other feel good. One way to make others feel good is to really listen to their ideas.

When I listen, I will give full attention to the other. I will trust there is some value in the ideas expressed and I will prepare my mind to accept the value of the ideas.

No matter how rushed I am, I will not judge the worth of the idea immediately. I will first acknowledge in a nonjudgmental way that I heard a reasonable idea. This acknowledgment shows the other that I really listened and helps the other feel good.

Personal Affirmations

I, (your name), help others feel good by really listening to their ideas.

You, (your name), help others feel good by really listening to their ideas.

(Your name) helps others feel good by really listening to their ideas.

We, (your name) and (other's name), help others feel good by really listening to their ideas.

Reciprocal Affirmations

I, (your name), help you feel good by really listening to your ideas.

You, (other's name), help me feel good by really listening to my ideas.

We, (your name) and (other's name), help each other feel good by really listening to each other's ideas.

(Your name) and (other's name) help each other feel good by really listening to each other's ideas.

We are so eager to have our relationships work that we sometimes forget ourselves. We become preoccupied with our responses to the other and the other's responses to us.

Our communication, love and connection with another are only as strong as our communication, love and connection with ourselves. We need to know and enjoy ourselves to share ourselves with others. Otherwise, we project mixed messages which confuse and complicate our relationships.

I can take time for myself to read, to enjoy the universe, to take a walk, to complete an enjoyable project and to cultivate and tone my body, mind and spirit.

Personal Affirmations

I, (your name), take time for myself independent of my relationships.

You, (your name), take time for yourself independent of your relationships.

(Your name) takes time for herself/himself independent of her/his relationships.

We, (your name) and (other's name), take time for ourselves independent of our relationships.

Reciprocal Affirmations

I, (your name), take time for myself independent of our relationship.

You, (other's name), take time for yourself independent of our relationship.

We, (your name) and (other's name), take time for ourselves independent of our relationship.

(Your name) and (other's name) take time for themselves independent of their relationship.

When I need to make a decision with another, I may assume there is only one right answer. It's easy, then, to argue that my favorite answer is the right one. In order to make choices that will work for us both, I need to accept that there is always more than one right answer or even two.

We need to discuss all our options without passing judgment on them to find out how we each feel about them. We need to think and listen with an open mind. Often good listening, to ourselves and others, removes the need for heavy or argumentative analysis. Our best joint answer becomes plain in the light of open communication.

Personal Affirmations

I, (your name), am receptive to a range of options.
You, (your name), are receptive to a range of options.
(Your name) is receptive to a range of options.
We, (your name) and (other's name), are receptive to a range of options.

Reciprocal Affirmations

I, (your name), am receptive to options you propose.
You, (other's name), are receptive to options I propose.
We, (your name) and (other's name), are receptive to options proposed by the other.
(Your name) and (other's name) are receptive to options proposed by the other.

In our eagerness to be loving and caring toward others, we can forget to consider what we really want ourselves. If the wants of others seem overwhelming or if we complain that others aren't clear about their demands on us, chances are we need to focus on our own wants.

Then we need to let others know our wants. It's not up to others to guess at our wants or figure out what we would appreciate most from them. It's up to us to ask for what we want.

I acknowledge the freedom of others to ignore my requests, but I acknowledge my freedom and responsibility to myself to ask for what I want.

Personal Affirmations

I, (your name), ask for what I want in my relationships.

You, (your name), ask for what you want in your relationships.

(Your name) asks for what she/he wants in her/his relationships.

We, (your name) and (other's name), ask for what we want in our relationships.

Reciprocal Affirmations

I, (your name), ask for what I want in our relationship.

You, (other's name), ask for what you want in our relationship.

We, (your name) and (other's name), ask for what we want in our relationship.

(Your name) and (other's name) ask for what they want in their relationship.

An important element of friendship is facing or sharing common challenges or concerns. This gives us the bond we need to feel comfortable with the other. If we don't have common challenges, we tend to grow apart.

When I share my current challenges with another, I give friendship a chance to blossom. When the other responds with similar challenges, our friendship is strengthened by the common concern. If the other doesn't have or appreciate a similar challenge, I will still feel good about expressing what I'm feeling.

Personal Affirmations

I, (your name), feel free to express my current challenges.

You, (your name), feel free to express your current challenges.

(Your name) feels free to express her/his current challenges.

We, (your name) and (other's name), feel free to express our current challenges.

Reciprocal Affirmations

I, (your name), feel free to express my current challenges to you.

You, (other's name), feel free to express your current challenges to me.

We, (your name) and (other's name), feel free to express our current challenges to each other.

(Your name) and (other's name) feel free to express their current challenges to each other.

When we feel we'll go bananas unless we make a change, we often hesitate to take the risk. We fear the risk of leaving our comfort zone making a change that will affect a relationship or both.

It's comforting to remember that change is inevitable and that the only constant is change. If we don't change ourselves, if we try to hang on and keep things the same, something will change anyway. It feels good to make positive changes that we choose, rather than changes that are imposed on us or just happen.

Personal Affirmations
I, (your name), accept the risk of positive changes.
You, (your name), accept the risk of positive changes.
(Your name) accepts the risk of positive changes.
We, (your name) and (other's name), accept the risk of positive changes.

Reciprocal Affirmations
I, (your name), accept the risk of positive changes.
You, (other's name), accept the risk of positive changes.
We, (your name) and (other's name), accept the risk of positive changes.
(Your name) and (other's name) accept the risk of positive changes.

Sometimes we are so involved in our multiple activities and responsibilities that we begin to feel wholly indispensable. It's nice to feel needed, but it becomes an intolerable burden when we feel the family, the organization and the universe cannot function without our full and constant dedication.

We need time off — to put our responsibilities in perspective, to build confidence in others to provide for themselves, to nurture our faith in the ongoing creative power of the universe and to renew our direction and energy. It's all right to let others help us and take care of us and serve us once in a while. Time off benefits us and those who rely on us.

Personal Affirmations

I, (your name), deserve a regular vacation from the
    norm.

You, (your name), deserve a regular vacation from the
    norm.

(Your name) deserves a regular vacation from the
    norm.

We, (your name) and (other's name), deserve a regular
    vacation from the norm.

Reciprocal Affirmations

I, (your name), deserve a regular vacation from the
    norm.

You, (other's name), deserve a regular vacation from
    the norm.

We, (your name) and (other's name), deserve a regular
    vacation from the norm.

(Your name) and (other's name) deserve a regular
    vacation from the norm.

We exert a great deal of influence in our relationships by our voice alone. We can improve the environment in which we interact merely by paying attention to how we use our voice.

Are we speaking fast, clipping our words? Are we using a whining tone? Are we talking loudly, even bombastically? Are we speaking inaudibly, hesitantly or hypnotically? Are we using an uneven pace, letting our voice crack, forgetting to breathe or letting our sentences drag on?

We might recall someone we've really enjoyed talking with and notice how they used their voice. Their voice may have had more influence on our relationship with them than we realized.

Personal Affirmations

I, (your name), use my voice wisely.

You, (your name), use your voice wisely.

(Your name) uses her/his voice wisely.

We, (your name) and (other's name), each use our voices wisely.

Reciprocal Affirmations

I, (your name), use my voice wisely with you.

You, (other's name), use your voice wisely with me.

We, (your name) and (other's name), use our voices wisely with each other.

(Your name) and (other's name) use their voices wisely with each other.

The key to success in strong, long-lasting relationships is found in three buzzwords — commitment,
communication and mutual support. A relationship can
only be strong and long-lasting if I am willing to put my
energy and enthusiasm into it, to commit myself to
making it work.

I need to give support and empathy to the other in a
relationship, just as I need to receive support and empathy from the other for the relationship to be a success.
And a relationship needs open and honest communication between the parties to be strong and successful.
Communication is necessary to mutual support and is
important for expressing commitment.

Personal Affirmations

I, (your name), give others commitment, communica-
    tion and mutual support.

You, (your name), give others commitment, communi-
    cation and mutual support.

(Your name) gives others commitment, communica-
    tion and mutual support.

We, (your name) and (other's name), give others com-
    mitment, communication and mutual support.

Reciprocal Affirmations

I, (your name), give you commitment, communication
    and mutual support.

You, (other's name), give me commitment, communi-
    cation and mutual support.

We, (your name) and (other's name), give each other
    commitment, communication and mutual support.

(Your name) and (other's name) give each other com-
    mitment, communication and mutual support.

Perhaps the most important relationship we have is the one with ourselves. Unless we have a good relationship with ourselves, one in which we like ourselves and which leads to high self-esteem, we will have a difficult time with others.

An honest look at what we like and don't like about ourselves is the first step to a good relationship with ourselves. Then we need to encourage the things we like and change the things we don't like. The more things we like about ourselves, the better our relationships will be.

Personal Affirmations

I, (your name), am improving my relationship with myself.

You, (your name), are improving your relationship with yourself.

(Your name) is improving her/his relationship with herself/himself.

We, (your name) and (other's name), are improving our relationships with ourselves.

Reciprocal Affirmations

I, (your name), am improving my relationship with myself.

You, (other's name), are improving your relationship with yourself.

We, (your name) and (other's name), are improving our relationships with ourselves.

(Your name) and (other's name) are improving their relationships with themselves.

There are many aspects to a healthy love relationship. Physical touching is an important one. Little expressions of affection, such as a touch, kiss or hug, can mean a lot to me and the other in a relationship. But perfunctory touches, kisses and hugs mean little.

I need to express my affection by making my touches, kisses and hugs heartfelt every time. These expressions of love can help partners feel closer to one another.

Personal Affirmations

I, (your name), take the time to give heartfelt touches, kisses and hugs.

You, (your name), take the time to give heartfelt touches, kisses and hugs.

(Your name) takes the time to give heartfelt touches, kisses and hugs.

We, (your name) and (other's name), take the time to give heartfelt touches, kisses and hugs.

Reciprocal Affirmations

I, (your name), take the time to give you heartfelt touches, kisses and hugs.

You, (other's name), take the time to give me heartfelt touches, kisses and hugs.

We, (your name) and (other's name), take the time to give each other heartfelt touches, kisses and hugs.

(Your name) and (other's name) take the time to give each other heartfelt touches, kisses and hugs.

Sometimes we struggle with situations beyond our control and our self-esteem suffers. We may feel ignorant and lacking in ability to make good decisions for ourselves. Yet we know deep down we want to make our own decisions and learn from our own mistakes.

This inner conflict can trouble our relationships. We may defer to others and accept a student's role, feeling bound to obey their advice and yet rebellious and resentful about their mentor status. We may even fight to become mentors ourselves.

In each relationship I may be a student for a time, but I always have the freedom to make my own decisions and to take or reject and give or withhold advice.

Personal Affirmations

I, (your name), choose whether to defer to others.
You, (your name), choose whether to defer to others.
(Your name) chooses whether to defer to others.
We, (your name) and (other's name), choose whether to defer to others.

Reciprocal Affirmations

I, (your name), choose whether to defer to you.
You, (other's name), choose whether to defer to me.
We, (your name) and (other's name), choose whether to defer to each other.
(Your name) and (other's name) choose whether to defer to each other.

In our relationships we need to consider our physical appearance. In a mass culture that pushes narrow concepts of beauty, it's easy to reject the physical as superficial and unimportant. Indeed we don't need to match up to Hollywood, *Vogue* or *GQ* to have our physical appearance reflect the beauty of our inner being.

But no matter what style we prefer, people will be more attracted to us if we have our skin and hair clean, keep nails and hair groomed, wear clean and neat clothing and avoid unpleasant odors from smoking, drinking, poor nutrition and poor dental care. Even those close to us relate to us better if we take good care of ourselves.

Personal Affirmations

I, (your name), take good care of my personal appearance.

You, (your name), take good care of your personal appearance.

(Your name) takes good care of her/his personal appearance.

We, (your name) and (other's name), take good care of our personal appearance.

Reciprocal Affirmations

I, (your name), take good care of my personal appearance.

You, (other's name), take good care of your personal appearance.

We, (your name) and (other's name), take good care of our personal appearance.

(Your name) and (other's name) take good care of their personal appearance.

While sometimes we're astounded at all the changes that happen in our lives, at other times we wonder why the changes we're trying to make seem to take forever. When desired changes are slow to happen, we need to be persistent.

Persistence is one part faith and one part hard-headed stubbornness. We need both the belief that the desired changes will happen and the stick-to-it-iveness to see them through until they do.

Personal Affirmations

I, (your name), am persistent with positive changes I seek.

You, (your name), are persistent with positive changes you seek.

(Your name) is persistent with positive changes she/he seeks.

We, (your name) and (other's name), are persistent with positive changes we seek.

Reciprocal Affirmations

I, (your name), am persistent with positive changes we seek.

You, (other's name), are persistent with positive changes we seek.

We, (your name) and (other's name), are persistent with positive changes we seek.

(Your name) and (other's name) are persistent with positive changes they seek.

Making joint decisions is a common stumbling block in relationships. The first step to success is recognizing the issue as one for a joint decision rather than the individual province of one party. The second step is communication. We won't be able to make a joint decision if one of us refuses to talk about the issue.

Once we're talking, how do we reach an agreement? The important thing is to agree on the result. It's not necessary to use the same thought processes, have the same reasons or have the same feelings about the outcome.

Personal Affirmations

I, (your name), focus on results in joint decision-making.

You, (your name), focus on results in joint decision-making.

(Your name) focuses on results in joint decision-making.

We, (your name) and (other's name), focus on results in joint decision-making.

Reciprocal Affirmations

I, (your name), focus on results in our decision-making.

You, (other's name), focus on results in our decision-making.

We, (your name) and (other's name), focus on results in our decision-making.

(Your name) and (other's name) focus on results in their decision-making.

In our joint decisions, sometimes we fall into a proposer and disposer pattern. One seems to have responsibility for coming up with ideas, while the other becomes judge of their ultimate merit. This habit of interaction becomes dry and unsatisfying with time.

Proposers may feel their ideas aren't given enough credence or that, if they had more say over the actual execution, the ideas could be made to work. They may grow resentful and tend to avoid joint decisions. Disposers may believe they could develop superior ideas if only they didn't have so many evaluative responsibilities. They may resent the creative expression the other seems to enjoy.

Try mutual brainstorming and shared evaluation processes instead.

Personal Affirmations
I, (your name), am both proposer and disposer.
You, (your name), are both proposer and disposer.
(Your name) is both proposer and disposer.
We, (your name) and (other's name), both propose and both dispose.

Reciprocal Affirmations
I, (your name), am both proposer and disposer.
You, (other's name), are both proposer and disposer.
We, (your name) and (other's name), both propose and both dispose.
(Your name) and (other's name) both propose and both dispose.

When we're angry or frustrated by events or people at work, we often behave in an angry or frustrated way at home. We carry the mood home, are sensitive and lash out at those close to us when any little thing doesn't go perfectly.

We need to learn to keep any anger and frustration out of the rest of our lives. Just because one area of our lives is a source of negative feelings, we don't have to make other areas unpleasant. We need to leave our anger and frustration where it arose and enjoy the love and companionship we have in other areas of our lives.

Personal Affirmations

I, (your name), leave any anger and frustration with work at work.

You, (your name), leave any anger and frustration with work at work.

(Your name) leaves any anger and frustration with work at work.

We, (your name) and (other's name), each leave any anger and frustration with work at work.

Reciprocal Affirmations

I, (your name), leave any anger and frustration with my work at work.

You, (other's name), leave any anger and frustration with your work at work.

We, (your name) and (other's name), each leave any anger and frustration with our work at work.

(Your name) and (other's name) each leave any anger and frustration with their work at work.

We each have unlimited power for good. If we feel trapped in a negative relationship, we may feel powerless to change our circumstances. But small positive changes within our power can bring about big changes in the way we feel about our lives. We might just change our tone of voice. Or we might let a careless accusation go unanswered. Or we might decline an unreasonable demand with grace rather than resentment.

The good results from small positive changes we make may at first seem like miracles. We need not believe in our power for good to experience it. We need only suspend our disbelief. Experience will teach us.

Personal Affirmations

I, (your name), am ready to experience my power for good.

You, (your name), are ready to experience your power for good.

(Your name) is ready to experience her/his power for good.

We, (your name) and (other's name), are ready to experience our power for good.

Reciprocal Affirmations

I, (your name), am ready to experience my power for good.

You, (other's name), are ready to experience your power for good.

We, (your name) and (other's name), are ready to experience our power for good.

(Your name) and (other's name) are ready to experience their power for good.

Along with food, shelter and clothing, meaningful relationships are a basic need. They deserve a position high on our priority list — above a promotion, a new car, a nicer vacation or a busier social life. If they drop too low in priority, all other accomplishments will feel empty and unrewarding. And after a time of neglecting basic needs, we even lose the power to accomplish other things.

If we focus on meeting not only our basic physical needs but also our spiritual need for enriching human relationships, we find contentment without a lot of extras. But curiously, extras still do come and we find it easier to enjoy them.

Personal Affirmations
I, (your name), give my relationships high priority.
You, (your name), give your relationships high priority.
(Your name) gives her/his relationships high priority.
We, (your name) and (other's name), give our relationships high priority.

Reciprocal Affirmations
I, (your name), give our relationship high priority.
You, (other's name), give our relationship high priority.
We, (your name) and (other's name), give our relationship high priority.
(Your name) and (other's name) give their relationship high priority.

Changing relationships takes courage. We fear the unknown. Our current situation is known, and no matter how bad, there is comfort in that. We fear that a change, a step into the unknown, could make things worse or more uncomfortable.

Overcoming fear of change can be a struggle. We need to look at what's at stake: improving the relationship. Isn't it worth a risk to improve relationships that affect us daily? Once we decide it's worth the risk, fear becomes a much smaller deterrent to change — one that's manageable.

Personal Affirmations
I, (your name), face change with courage.
You, (your name), face change with courage.
(Your name) faces change with courage.
We, (your name) and (other's name), face change
with courage.

Reciprocal Affirmations
I, (your name), face change with courage.
You, (other's name), face change with courage.
We, (your name) and (other's name), face change
with courage.
(Your name) and (other's name) face change with
courage.

We often go into a relationship unsure of what to expect. We wonder if our feelings, hopes and dreams are shared. We are insecure about the other's intentions.

If we share our expectations with the other, we can find out where we stand. Equally important, we will have started a dialogue about our relationship. Through this dialogue we can each express our expectations, hopes and dreams for the relationship. We can discover common expectations and set goals. Through communication we can guide our relationship.

Personal Affirmations

I, (your name), share my expectations.
You, (your name), share your expectations.
(Your name) shares her/his expectations.
We, (your name) and (other's name), share our expectations.

Reciprocal Affirmations

I, (your name), share my expectations with you.
You, (other's name), share your expectations with me.
We, (your name) and (other's name), share our expectations with each other.
(Your name) and (other's name) share their expectations with each other.

Where did I learn about relationships? Most of what I learned was from observing the relationships in my home as I grew up. Whether they were good examples that have served me well or poor examples that have led me into difficulty, it's important for me to realize I am free to choose different relationship patterns.

I don't have to continue to relate the way I learned by example as a child. I recognize that the pattern I learned is only one of many. I am letting go of old relationship patterns and establishing patterns that are healthy for me.

Personal Affirmations

I, (your name), can choose different relationship patterns.

You, (your name), can choose different relationship patterns.

(Your name) can choose different relationship patterns.

We, (your name) and (other's name), can choose different relationship patterns.

Reciprocal Affirmations

I, (your name), can choose a different relationship pattern.

You, (other's name), can choose a different relationship pattern.

We, (your name) and (other's name), can choose a different relationship pattern.

(Your name) and (other's name) can choose a different relationship pattern.

Flexibility nurtures the health of our relationships. Often our daily routine, everyday habits and patterns of thought need to be re-examined and adjusted to new circumstances in our lives. Our wants and needs are inevitably changing as our relationships develop and our lives unfold.

Much of the friction that develops in our relationships can be overcome by a personal "sunset law." We need to regularly review our routines, habits and patterns of thought to see if they still serve us well or would be better abandoned or changed. This isn't an admission of wrong in the past, only a recognition that things change and we need to be flexible and open to growth.

Personal Affirmations

I, (your name), regularly review and adjust my routines.

You, (your name), regularly review and adjust your routines.

(Your name) regularly reviews and adjusts her/his routines.

We, (your name) and (other's name), regularly review and adjust our routines.

Reciprocal Affirmations

I, (your name), regularly review and adjust my routines.

You, (other's name), regularly review and adjust your routines.

We, (your name) and (other's name), regularly review and adjust our routines.

(Your name) and (other's name) regularly review and adjust their routines.

Our analytical skills have an important place in our lives. We use them to judge information and perhaps our own actions and words.

But it's a mistake to judge people. That's a task fit only for the Creator. We need to accept the worth of ourselves and others without passing judgment. Even with our flaws and foibles, we are all worthwhile as people and deserve unconditional love.

Personal Affirmations

I, (your name), accept the worth of myself and others without passing judgment.

You, (your name), accept the worth of yourself and others without passing judgment.

(Your name) accepts the worth of herself/himself and others without passing judgment.

We, (your name) and (other's name), accept the worth of ourselves and others without passing judgment.

Reciprocal Affirmations

I, (your name), accept your worth without passing judgment.

You, (other's name), accept my worth without passing judgment.

We, (your name) and (other's name), accept each other's worth without passing judgment.

(Your name) and (other's name) accept each other's worth without passing judgment.

Are you grumpy when you have the flu or a cold? When we're well-rested, not sick and have just exercised, we feel happy, healthy, strong and vigorous. We radiate and communicate our health and well-being to all those around us. Therefore our health has a significant effect on our relationships.

We need to guard our health and do the things necessary to achieve and maintain vigorous good health. Our outlook and relationships improve to the extent we are healthy.

Personal Affirmations
I, (your name), improve my health and relationships
    together.
You, (your name), improve your health and relation-
    ships together.
(Your name) improves her/his health and relationships
    together.
We, (your name) and (other's name), improve our
    health and relationships together.

Reciprocal Affirmations
I, (your name), improve my health and relationship
    with you.
You, (other's name), improve your health and relation-
    ship with me.
We, (your name) and (other's name), improve our
    health and our relationship.
(Your name) and (other's name) improve their health
    and their relationship.

When we live with another, we easily take on many duties and responsibilities for our life together. We may go out of our way to please the other. If the other doesn't seem to notice, we may feel unappreciated. Then we tend to blame the other for making us feel that way and overreact to any negative remarks or additional requests.

But there are better ways to overcome resentment. I can examine the things I do and let go of those I cannot do comfortably without thought of reward. I can find new ways to appreciate myself. And I can acknowledge my value and that of the other by expressing my feelings without placing blame.

Personal Affirmations

I, (your name), appreciate myself and my feelings.

You, (your name), appreciate yourself and your feelings.

(Your name) appreciates herself/himself and her/his feelings.

We, (your name) and (other's name), each appreciate ourselves and our own feelings.

Reciprocal Affirmations

I, (your name), appreciate myself and my feelings.

You, (other's name), appreciate yourself and your feelings.

We, (your name) and (other's name), each appreciate ourselves and our own feelings.

(Your name) and (other's name) each appreciate themselves and their own feelings.

The sexual aspect of a relationship changes and grows just like other aspects. The idea that sex is simply satisfying or unsatisfying, good or bad, orgasmic or not, ignores the fact that sex is a form of communication. It's the ultimate expression of physical sharing. In its purest form sex creates an actual exchange of body fluids, just as speech in its purest form creates an exchange of thoughts.

The frequency, intensity, timing, enjoyment, tenderness and satisfaction of sex will vary depending on the vitality and immediate needs of the relationship. Taking responsibility for my own sexual response and being honest with my partner about my sexual needs and wants will help our sexual relationship grow.

Personal Affirmations

I, (your name), take responsibility for my sexual growth.

You, (your name), take responsibility for your sexual growth.

(Your name) takes responsibility for her/his sexual growth.

We, (your name) and (other's name), each take responsibility for our own sexual growth.

Reciprocal Affirmations

I, (your name), let you take responsibility for your sexual growth.

You, (other's name), let me take responsibility for my sexual growth.

We, (your name) and (other's name), each take responsibility for our own sexual growth.

(Your name) and (other's name) each take responsibility for their own sexual growth.

It's difficult for people with very different value systems to have a successful long-term relationship. Perhaps you've noticed that people from similar backgrounds are more often successful with a long-term relationship than people from different backgrounds.

People from similar backgrounds learned common values at home, school, church and through similar experiences. They understand, perhaps intuitively, a similar value system, so they understand what motivates the other.

People who have different value systems can learn from this. If we search for our common values, we can relate more easily in those areas. This gives us a foundation for growth in our relationship.

Personal Affirmations
I, (your name), look for values I share with others.
You, (your name), look for values you share with others.
(Your name) looks for values she/he shares with others.
We, (your name) and (other's name), look for values
we share with others.

Reciprocal Affirmations
I, (your name), look for values I share with you.
You, (other's name), look for values you share with me.
We, (your name) and (other's name), look for values
we share.
(Your name) and (other's name) look for values they
share.

In a relationship we are wise to cultivate patience. Not the begrudging, tap-your-foot kind of patience we may have received from some adults when we were kids that made us feel small and inadequate. Rather, the kind of cheerful patience that shows respect for the other, their individuality and their right to make their own decisions.

We most often get impatient when we want or expect something from someone. We will inspire more cooperation and positive responses if we express our wants and expectations and then let them go, giving the other the freedom to respond in their own good time.

Personal Affirmations

I, (your name), am cheerfully patient with others.

You, (your name), are cheerfully patient with others.

(Your name) is cheerfully patient with others.

We, (your name) and (other's name), are cheerfully patient with others.

Reciprocal Affirmations

I, (your name), am cheerfully patient with you.

You, (other's name), are cheerfully patient with me.

We, (your name) and (other's name), are cheerfully patient with each other.

(Your name) and (other's name) are cheerfully patient with each other.

When others share their problems with us, we often jump in with both feet to find solutions. Each person has the power to resolve their own problems if they seek help from those who have superior experience or knowledge. But we are least likely to be able to help those close to us in this way. With those we hold close, we can help most by quiet listening and supportive affirmation. If we remain detached from the anxiety and worry of our loved ones, we can maintain our strength to be a shelter from the storm.

Personal Affirmations
I, (your name), don't worry about other people's problems.

You, (your name), don't worry about other people's problems.

(Your name) doesn't worry about other people's problems.

We, (your name) and (other's name), don't worry about other people's problems.

Reciprocal Affirmations
I, (your name), don't worry about your problems.

You, (other's name), don't worry about my problems.

We, (your name) and (other's name), don't worry about each other's problems.

(Your name) and (other's name) don't worry about each other's problems.

Just *being* can make us feel good. Being is a vacation from doing or accomplishing. Being focuses on the here and now and living this moment for itself. It is not learning information to use another time, nor figuring out if what another says today is consistent with what they said last week and not analyzing.

We can enjoy others while just being. We can enjoy their uniqueness and individuality without having our mental computer work overtime. Without thinking how it relates to the past or the future, we can just be happy with each moment.

Personal Affirmations
I, (your name), enjoy each moment for itself.
You, (your name), enjoy each moment for itself.
(Your name) enjoys each moment for itself.
We, (your name) and (other's name), enjoy each moment for itself.

Reciprocal Affirmations
I, (your name), enjoy each moment for itself.
You, (other's name), enjoy each moment for itself.
We, (your name) and (other's name), enjoy each moment for itself.
(Your name) and (other's name) enjoy each moment for itself.

It's easy to get overly analytical with people we love. Often we hear of or have had relationships that seem fun and rewarding at first but begin to stagnate when one member gets serious. When we begin to feel we have a personal stake in the other, we can lose the spontaneity and easy acceptance that make casual relationships enjoyable.

Instead of trying to figure them out, advise them, judge them, make them predictable or keep them consistent with our image of them, we need to give those we love space to be themselves. As they reveal themselves to us, we can enjoy their uniqueness and individuality without fear or judgment.

Personal Affirmations

I, (your name), enjoy the uniqueness of my partner.

You, (your name), enjoy the uniqueness of your partner.

(Your name) enjoys the uniqueness of her/his partner.

We, (your name) and (other's name), enjoy each other's uniqueness.

Reciprocal Affirmations

I, (your name), enjoy your uniqueness.

You, (other's name), enjoy my uniqueness.

We, (your name) and (other's name), enjoy each other's uniqueness.

(Your name) and (other's name) enjoy each other's uniqueness.

When we speak, those close to us hear on many levels. They recognize almost instantly if our words are humorous, defensive, exaggerated, informational, and so forth. But their minds still register the literal meaning for a moment. If the literal meaning is unacceptable or unrealistic, they can set it aside quickly, almost unknowingly. But the more often we use put-downs, sarcasm, exaggerations or angry words, the more worn the listeners' selective powers can become and the more defensive, reactive and angry their responses will be.

If we want genuine communication from those close to us, we need to think a moment about our choice of words before we speak.

Personal Affirmations
I, (your name), think before I speak.
You, (your name), think before you speak.
(Your name) thinks before she/he speaks.
We, (your name) and (other's name), think before we speak.

Reciprocal Affirmations
I, (your name), think before I speak to you.
You, (other's name), think before you speak to me.
We, (your name) and (other's name), think before we speak.
(Your name) and (other's name) think before they speak.

It takes courage to make a decision. Even the smallest decision involves risk. Someone may not understand your reasons, may judge you inappropriately or may perceive you inaccurately based on your decision. Even what pin to wear, whether to skip a shower to make an appointment or whether to write "Sincerely yours" or "Cordially yours" can raise fears and doubts in our minds.

In our relationships, we need to maintain our silence when the other is making such decisions of personal style. If we are used to always offering our advice, we need to let go, stop meddling and let them know we will not be judge and jury — that we admire their courage and respect their personal style.

Personal Affirmations

I, (your name), respect others' right to their personal
    style.
You, (your name), respect others' right to their personal
    style.
(Your name) respects others' right to their personal style.
We, (your name) and (other's name), respect others'
    right to their personal style.

Reciprocal Affirmations

I, (your name), respect your right to your personal
    style.
You, (other's name), respect my right to my personal
    style.
We, (your name) and (other's name), respect each
    other's right to their personal style.
(Your name) and (other's name) respect each other's
    right to their personal style.

Romance! I get warm feelings just thinking about the word. Romantic love is when I get a good feeling touching or being near my lover, giving something of myself, whispering sweet nothings to my lover or enjoying passion.

Romantic love isn't thinking my lover is perfect, that I should sacrifice myself, my desires or my career for my lover or that my lover should sacrifice them for me.

Romantic love, as all love, is strong and true when both my lover and I are whole people independent of our love relationship.

Personal Affirmations

I, (your name), can be romantic and still have my feet on the ground.

You, (your name), can be romantic and still have your feet on the ground.

(Your name) can be romantic and still have her/his feet on the ground.

We, (your name) and (other's name), can be romantic and still have our feet on the ground.

Reciprocal Affirmations

I, (your name), love you.

You, (other's name), love me.

We, (your name) and (other's name), love each other.

(Your name) and (other's name) love each other.

Each of us has suffered pain in the past. If we feel depressed, overburdened or weak, it's easy to resurrect that pain and use it to nurture self-pity. We may expect our partner to listen endlessly to our painful recountings and give us the sympathy we missed long ago.

But we need to remember that the other has their own pain. Each person's pain is their own. Sympathetic partners will not encourage us to wallow in self-pity. They will respond lovingly when we say we hurt. But they will be bored if we continually call on them to help us suppress our pain. It's our own job to work toward permanent release of our pain.

Personal Affirmations

I, (your name), don't overburden my partner with my pain.

You, (your name), don't overburden your partner with your pain.

(Your name) doesn't overburden her/his partner with her/his pain.

We, (your name) and (other's name), don't overburden others with our pain.

Reciprocal Affirmations

I, (your name), don't overburden you with my pain.

You, (other's name), don't overburden me with your pain.

We, (your name) and (other's name), don't overburden each other with our pain.

(Your name) and (other's name) don't overburden each other with their pain.

If we often feel angry at others, we may carry a personal source of anger. Many of us carry a deep anger at ourselves. Perhaps we are angry that we weren't able to get the love we deserved as children. Or that we've spent much of our lives worrying about or trying to help someone who didn't want our help. Or that we have put others' dreams ahead of our own.

We need to let go of this self-anger if we want to control angry outbursts at others. The first step is to accept that we did the best we could as children. We never could have controlled anyone else, no matter what we might have done.

Personal Affirmations

I, (your name), let go of anger at myself or my inner child.

You, (your name), let go of anger at yourself or your inner child.

(Your name) lets go of anger at herself/himself or her/his inner child.

We, (your name) and (other's name), let go of any anger at ourselves.

Reciprocal Affirmations

I, (your name), let go of anger at myself or my inner child.

You, (other's name), let go of anger at yourself or your inner child.

We, (your name) and (other's name), let go of any anger at ourselves.

(Your name) and (other's name) let go of any anger at themselves.

Remember the tremendous energy we put into establishing a relationship? We willingly use lots of energy
attracting, courting and securing a commitment from a
mate. But do we continue with anything approaching
that level of energy after the marriage or move-in? Or
do we turn to other areas of our lives with that energy?

Commitment to a relationship means not taking it for
granted once the relationship is established. Commitment means putting positive energy into nurturing a
relationship, supporting the other, loving, having fun
and spending time together. A successful relationship
doesn't just happen; it requires continual commitment.

Personal Affirmations

I, (your name), commit lots of positive energy to my
   relationship.

You, (your name), commit lots of positive energy to
   your relationship.

(Your name) commits lots of positive energy to her/his
   relationship.

We, (your name) and (other's name), commit lots of
   positive energy to our relationship.

Reciprocal Affirmations

I, (your name), commit lots of positive energy to our
   relationship.

You, (other's name), commit lots of positive energy to
   our relationship.

We, (your name) and (other's name), commit lots of
   positive energy to our relationship.

(Your name) and (other's name) commit lots of positive energy to their relationship.

When we share parenting with another, we need to recognize there are three relationships involved, only two of which are our business. So often we pass judgment on how our spouse or former spouse is relating to our child. Then we may try to make up for it in our own relationship with the child or heap criticisms on the other parent, until one or both of our relationships are compromised.

So long as our child is safe from actual injury by another parent, we do best by concentrating our efforts on improving the quality of our direct relationships with the child and the other parent. Our greatest positive effect on their relationship comes from our loving example.

Personal Affirmations

I, (your name), focus on my own parenting and not another's.

You, (your name), focus on your own parenting and not another's.

(Your name) focuses on her/his own parenting and not another's.

We, (your name) and (other's name), each focus on our own parenting and not the other's.

Reciprocal Affirmations

I, (your name), focus on my own parenting and not yours.

You, (other's name), focus on your own parenting and not mine.

We, (your name) and (other's name), each focus on our own parenting and not the other's.

(Your name) and (other's name) each focus on their own parenting and not the other's.

Sometimes in our relationships we expect the other to know how we feel. We think they should be so close, so much like us or so attentive that they can guess our feelings. But seldom will they know or guess correctly. Nor is it their responsibility or even right to do so. Each of us is responsible for our own feelings and the needs and wants they express.

I need to learn to share my feelings. Before I resort to complaining, self-pity, or accusations of thoughtlessness, let me make sure I have communicated my feelings. I will try to say more often, "I feel . . . overworked, joyous, warm, cool, unappreciated, eager" or whatever it may be.

Personal Affirmations

I, (your name), tell others how I feel.
You, (your name), tell others how you feel.
(Your name) tells others how she/he feels.
We, (your name) and (other's name), tell others how we feel.

Reciprocal Affirmations

I, (your name), tell you how I feel.
You, (other's name), tell me how you feel.
We, (your name) and (other's name), tell each other how we feel.
(Your name) and (other's name) tell each other how they feel.

I really enjoy the times I'm smiling and cheerful. But the times I'm depressed aren't so great. Have we noticed how our mind and body get on the same wavelength? If one is happy, the other is, and vice versa.

To smile and be cheerful takes — what? — the mind or the body to lead the other to the happy wavelength. Even if I'm down, a smile on the physical level helps put a smile on the mental level and brings me out of depression to cheerfulness.

Personal Affirmations

I, (your name), cheer myself out of depression with smiles.

You, (your name), cheer yourself out of depression with smiles.

(Your name) cheers herself/himself out of depression with smiles.

We, (your name) and (other's name), cheer ourselves out of depression with smiles.

Reciprocal Affirmations

I, (your name), cheer myself out of depression with smiles.

You, (other's name), cheer yourself out of depression with smiles.

We, (your name) and (other's name), cheer ourselves out of depression with smiles.

(Your name) and (other's name) cheer themselves out of depression with smiles.

Life presents each of us with a series of challenges, problems or opportunities for growth. These may or may not be the same or similar to those faced at the same time by another we have a relationship with. We must deal with our own challenges but resist managing or solving the other person's problems.

We can offer the other only empathy. Others need to come up with their own solutions for reasons of self-esteem. Only then will they feel good enough about themselves to carry through and solve their problems.

Personal Affirmations

I, (your name), offer empathy to others.

You, (your name), offer empathy to others.

(Your name) offers empathy to others.

We, (your name) and (other's name), offer others empathy.

Reciprocal Affirmations

I, (your name), offer you empathy.

You, (other's name), offer me empathy.

We, (your name) and (other's name), offer each other empathy.

(Your name) and (other's name) offer each other empathy.

Before we can relate well to another, we must relate to ourselves. Before we can be good to another, we need to be good to ourselves. Before we can help another, we must help ourselves. Before we can find the good in another, we must find the good in ourselves.

To love another, we must love ourselves. This isn't selfish in the old negative sense. We don't indulge ourselves at the expense of others or fill our needs while disregarding the needs of others. Instead, we appreciate that each follows their own path. If we aren't attending to our path, we cannot be serene and secure enough to share our path with another.

Personal Affirmations

I, (your name), tend to my needs without fear of self-ishness.

You, (your name), tend to your needs without fear of selfishness.

(Your name) tends to her/his needs without fear of selfishness.

We, (your name) and (other's name), each tend to our own needs without fear of selfishness.

Reciprocal Affirmations

I, (your name), tend to my needs without fear of self-ishness.

You, (other's name), tend to your needs without fear of selfishness.

We, (your name) and (other's name), each tend to our own needs without fear of selfishness.

(Your name) and (other's name) each tend to their own needs without fear of selfishness.

We all get angry from time to time. It's a normal, natural emotion. Anger itself isn't anything to be ashamed of, although much angry behavior is. How can we express the natural emotion of anger in an acceptable way?

The first step is acknowledging our anger. "I'm angry about that. I'm really angry that such and such happened." Acknowledging lets us know we are angry, and, just as important, what we are angry about. This prevents the touchy powder-keg syndrome, where any little thing can provoke an explosion. It also keeps the anger focused on the anger-producing situation and helps prevent our anger from being taken out on others.

Personal Affirmations

I, (your name), acknowledge my anger and what it's about.

You, (your name), acknowledge your anger and what it's about.

(Your name) acknowledges her/his anger and what it's about.

We, (your name) and (other's name), acknowledge our anger and what it's about.

Reciprocal Affirmations

I, (your name), acknowledge my anger and what it's about.

You, (other's name), acknowledge your anger and what it's about.

We, (your name) and (other's name), acknowledge our anger and what it's about.

(Your name) and (other's name) acknowledge their anger and what it's about.

Sometimes we have different rules for those close to us and for other people. Because we care more about them, we try harder to make them better, to correct their errors, to keep them on the straight and narrow, to make them worthy of our love.

But those we love need to be the primary targets for the understanding and acceptance we try to give others. Our home should be a haven of peace and understanding. If we nurture and project these attitudes, we will discover — perhaps to our surprise — that our loved ones will not fall apart or otherwise disappoint us. Understanding breeds understanding.

Personal Affirmations

I, (your name), make my home a haven of peace.
You, (your name), make your home a haven of peace.
(Your name) makes her/his home a haven of peace.
We, (your name) and (other's name), make our home
   a haven of peace.

Reciprocal Affirmations

I, (your name), make our home a haven of peace.
You, (other's name), make our home a haven of peace.
We, (your name) and (other's name), make our home
   a haven of peace.
(Your name) and (other's name) make their home a
   haven of peace.

Money is a frequent cause of upsets in a relationship. Sometimes we get bent out of shape over the way the other spent some money. We feel upset because we've been trying to do without, avoided using credit or tried to save money.

We need to respond nonjudgmentally and with trust, and get in touch with our righteousness or martyrdom. We can't judge what the other needs, either physically or psychologically. We must trust their judgment of what's best for them and let them make their own mistakes. (That's the only way they learn.) Maybe what our reaction really tells us is that we've misjudged ourselves, that our feelings of righteousness or martyrdom mean we have unfulfilled needs of our own.

Personal Affirmations

I, (your name), trust others to make their own spending decisions.

You, (your name), trust others to make their own spending decisions.

(Your name) trusts others to make their own spending decisions.

We, (your name) and (other's name), trust others' spending decisions.

Reciprocal Affirmations

I, (your name), trust you to make your own spending decisions.

You, (other's name), trust me to make my own spending decisions.

We, (your name) and (other's name), trust each other's spending decisions.

(Your name) and (other's name) trust each other's spending decisions.

Humor helps us in serious matters. When we can
look at something we have done and laugh compas-
sionately, we forgive ourselves for well-meant but ignorant behavior. When we laugh with someone else, we
do the same for them. We help lighten their load. We
acknowledge our common humanity.

Don't be afraid to smile when another is tormented.
We need not take on their emotion, only listen and
hear it. We must avoid making light of their problem.
We need instead the kind of humor that acknowledges
the seriousness of their challenge and the intensity of
their emotion but at the same time puts it in a human
perspective. We need the smile that says, "I, too, have
been there."

Personal Affirmations

I, (your name), maintain my humor in serious matters.
You, (your name), maintain your humor in serious
*   matters.*
(Your name) maintains her/his humor in serious
*   matters.*
We, (your name) and (other's name), maintain our
*   humor in serious matters.*

Reciprocal Affirmations

I, (your name), maintain my humor in serious matters.
You, (other's name), maintain your humor in serious
*   matters.*
We, (your name) and (other's name), maintain our
*   humor in serious matters.*
(Your name) and (other's name) maintain their
*   humor in serious matters.*

Sexual intimacy can be one of the greatest joys in the universe. The moment when we reach oneness at orgasm or both reach it at the same time through simultaneous orgasm is perhaps the greatest pleasure known to mankind. The unity, closeness and satisfaction are extreme.

Reaching this level of intimacy is often inhibited by anxieties and a goal orientation. We need to be intimate in a relaxed way, without anxiety and without trying to over-control the course of any one event. Only then will our sexual energies flow naturally to help us achieve the ultimate.

Personal Affirmations
I, (your name), am intimate without anxiety.
You, (your name), are intimate without anxiety.
(Your name) is intimate without anxiety.
We, (your name) and (other's name), are intimate
without anxiety.

Reciprocal Affirmations
I, (your name), am intimate without anxiety.
You, (other's name), are intimate without anxiety.
We, (your name) and (other's name), are intimate
without anxiety.
(Your name) and (other's name) are intimate without
anxiety.

Do we feel there is enough joy in our lives? In our relationships? How about love? Or money? The universe has an infinite abundance of joy, love and wealth. There is plenty for each of us. Our joy doesn't diminish the joy of anyone else. On the contrary, each joyful person increases the joy of others. So it is with love and money and all other positive qualities.

The feeling of sharing in the abundance of the universe is called prosperity. We deserve to be prosperous in all things.

Personal Affirmations

I, (your name), share in the abundance of the universe.

You, (your name), share in the abundance of the universe.

(Your name) shares in the abundance of the universe.

We, (your name) and (other's name), share in the abundance of the universe.

Reciprocal Affirmations

I, (your name), share in the abundance of the universe.

You, (other's name), share in the abundance of the universe.

We, (your name) and (other's name), share in the abundance of the universe.

(Your name) and (other's name) share in the abundance of the universe.

Competitiveness gets in the way of building "buddy" relationships. It's unlikely we are actually competing with our buddy for the same date or the same promotion. It's likely our competition is image competition — I'm more beautiful or macho or have more money. We need to set aside competition with our buddies if we want to deepen our relationships with them.

In our buddy relationships we want to get beyond image to a deeper level. This gives us a reason for letting go of image competition to build the relationship.

Personal Affirmations

I, (your name), set aside image competition to build relationships.

You, (your name), set aside image competition to build relationships.

(Your name) sets aside image competition to build relationships.

We, (your name) and (other's name), set aside image competition to build relationships.

Reciprocal Affirmations

I, (your name), set aside image competition to build my relationships.

You, (other's name), set aside image competition to build your relationships.

We, (your name) and (other's name), set aside image competition to build relationships.

(Your name) and (other's name) set aside image competition to build relationships.

If we share our economic life with another, we need to be willing to assert our needs and wants. If we are reluctant to spend money on ourselves or to ask for it, we can become resentful and self-righteous. But it's not the other's problem or concern if we martyr ourselves and justify it as parsimoniousness. It's our problem alone.

Rather than criticize the other for spending money on their desires, we need to get to know what spending choices we are comfortable with ourselves and begin to assert them. Rather than comparing and competing, we need to take responsibility for our own spending behavior.

Personal Affirmations

I, (your name), take responsibility for spending money for myself.

You, (your name), take responsibility for spending money for yourself.

(Your name) takes responsibility for spending money for herself/himself.

We, (your name) and (other's name), each take responsibility for spending money for ourselves.

Reciprocal Affirmations

I, (your name), take responsibility for spending money for myself.

You, (other's name), take responsibility for spending money for yourself.

We, (your name) and (other's name), each take responsibility for spending money for ourselves.

(Your name) and (other's name) each take responsibility for spending money for themselves.

Sometimes we think the only way to get the acceptance and understanding we want is to have someone else see things our way. We may have cultivated our power of persuasion, our logic and our reason. We may even be skilled at talking people into things and making them comfortable with new ideas.

To have our ideas accepted is indeed a comforting feeling. But if we are dependent upon it for our self-esteem, it will get in the way of our relationships. We pursue arguments ad infinitum, each molehill becomes a mountain and we refuse to let a matter drop. Even with those close to us, we must at times agree to disagree.

Personal Affirmations

I, (your name), feel good about agreeing to disagree.
You, (your name), feel good about agreeing to disagree.
(Your name) feels good about agreeing to disagree.
We, (your name) and (other's name), feel good about agreeing to disagree.

Reciprocal Affirmations

I, (your name), feel good about agreeing to disagree.
You, (other's name), feel good about agreeing to disagree.
We, (your name) and (other's name), feel good about agreeing to disagree.
(Your name) and (other's name) feel good about agreeing to disagree.

When I have a good relationship I will celebrate it, not take it for granted. A celebration is a reward I share with the other. It's support for our relationship.

A celebration is a fun time to remind ourselves of the fun and good times we have together and the joy of our relationship. It's also a time for renewal, a reaffirmation of the commitment, communication and mutual support that have made our relationship a success.

The celebration can be a special dinner or activity or just a special time set aside to reflect, to communicate our pleasure with our successes in the relationship and to recommit ourselves to the relationship.

Personal Affirmations

I, (your name), celebrate my relationships.
You, (your name), celebrate your relationships.
(Your name) celebrates her/his relationships.
We, (your name) and (other's name), celebrate our relationships.

Reciprocal Affirmations

I, (your name), celebrate our relationship.
You, (other's name), celebrate our relationship.
We, (your name) and (other's name), celebrate our relationship.
(Your name) and (other's name) celebrate their relationship.

If we try too hard not to look foolish, silly or stupid, we often settle for mediocrity in our affairs. As children, we may have been urged to "think before we speak" and consider "What will people think?" before we acted. This useful advice is overdone when it makes us fearful of others' impressions. We know intuitively it's human to look silly at times, and we become preoccupied with controlling what others think of us rather than with our own words and actions.

Our relationships slowly lose their energy when we tend to take the safe habitual course to maintain control. Instead we must be ourselves and let the chips fall where they may.

Personal Affirmations

I, (your name), am not fearful of what others think of me.

You, (your name), aren't fearful of what others think of you.

(Your name) isn't fearful of what others think of her/ him.

We, (your name) and (other's name), aren't fearful of what others think of us.

Reciprocal Affirmations

I, (your name), am not fearful of what you think of me.

You, (other's name), aren't fearful of what I think of you.

We, (your name) and (other's name), aren't fearful of what the other thinks of us.

(Your name) and (other's name) aren't fearful of what the other thinks of them.

When people give us advice, do we feel we should follow it? Do we feel guilty if we don't?

No matter who the person is — our spouse, mother, father, brother, sister, best friend, boss or anyone else — they aren't us and don't know what's best for us. They may know what would be best for them in circumstances they believe are similar to ours, but they can't know what's best for us in our unique situation.

We can consider the advice of others if we want, but we don't have to. Then we can make our own decision and act on it without guilt.

Personal Affirmations

I, (your name), consider others' advice but make my own decisions.

You, (your name), consider others' advice but make your own decisions.

(Your name) considers others' advice but makes her/his own decisions.

We, (your name) and (other's name), consider others' advice but make our own decisions.

Reciprocal Affirmations

I, (your name), consider your advice but make my own decisions.

You, (other's name), consider my advice but make your own decisions.

We, (your name) and (other's name), consider each other's advice but each make our own decisions.

(Your name) and (other's name) consider each other's advice but each make their own decisions.

When we're busy or preoccupied we frequently view an interruption by another as a pain. We try to discourage the interruption by giving it as little attention as possible. As a result, the other is unsatisfied with our communication or keeps after us until they are satisfied, making for a long and painful exchange for both.

If we respond to the interruption as if the other has an important reason to talk to us, we can often shorten the interruption. By giving our full attention to the other, we shorten the exchange, let the other feel important and let both of us feel good about the communication.

Personal Affirmations

I, (your name), give my full attention when others address me.

You, (your name), give your full attention when others address you.

(Your name) gives her/his full attention when others address her/him.

We, (your name) and (other's name), give our full attention when others address us.

Reciprocal Affirmations

I, (your name), give my full attention when you address me.

You, (other's name), give your full attention when I address you.

We, (your name) and (other's name), give our full attention when the other addresses us.

(Your name) and (other's name) give their full attention when the other addresses them.

Regular, vigorous exercise is essential for good health. We've all heard that. Physical exercise makes us feel better and makes our bodies work better and more efficiently. It relieves stress, makes our minds clearer and allows us to focus and concentrate more easily. We've all heard these benefits and many of us have experienced them at one time or another. So why don't we all exercise regularly?

Self-esteem. We aren't giving ourselves high enough priority to take the time and effort to exercise for ourselves. We put our own needs so far down the list that we don't get to them. We must love ourselves enough to care for ourselves and how we feel and to start exercising.

Personal Affirmations

I, (your name), exercise for health.
You, (your name), exercise for health.
(Your name) exercises for health.
We, (your name) and (other's name), each exercise for health.

Reciprocal Affirmations

I, (your name), respect your time to exercise for health.
You, (other's name), respect my time to exercise for health.
We, (your name) and (other's name), each exercise for health.
(Your name) and (other's name) each exercise for health.

Sometimes we mistake daydreams for visions. We may convince ourselves we have a lot in common with our partner because we both dream of the same things — a similar home, similar vacations, similar social life or similar future for the world.

But a daydream can be a mere escape from reality, a flight of imagination that ends with no impact on everyday life. A vision, in contrast, is a compelling motivator toward change, a look at the possible future rather than at an imaginary world. For dreams to become visions, we must cultivate not only our imaginations, but also our shared beliefs, commitment and energy.

Personal Affirmations

I, (your name), cultivate my best dreams into visions for my future.

You, (your name), cultivate your best dreams into visions for your future.

(Your name) cultivates her/his best dreams into visions for her/his future.

We, (your name) and (other's name), cultivate our best dreams into visions for our future.

Reciprocal Affirmations

I, (your name), cultivate my best dreams into visions for our future.

You, (other's name), cultivate your best dreams into visions for our future.

We, (your name) and (other's name), cultivate our best dreams into visions for our future.

(Your name) and (other's name) cultivate their best dreams into visions for their future.

Each of us feels alone from time to time. We have particular challenges in our lives that we feel only we can overcome or even understand. We each have a unique bundle of concerns, hopes, triumphs and regrets. We each must ultimately live our own lives and bear responsibility for our own happiness.

Luckily we have two excellent tools to manage this aloneness. First, we can develop a conscious awareness of our direct connection to the universe, through traditional religion or any other spiritual path that helps us feel part of a larger whole. Second, we can share our feelings with another. Talking about it with someone else ends the feeling of being alone.

Personal Affirmations

I, (your name), am not alone — love is all around me.

You, (your name), aren't alone — love is all around you.

(Your name) isn't alone — love is all around her/him.

We, (your name) and (other's name), aren't alone — love is all around us.

Reciprocal Affirmations

I, (your name), am not alone — love is all around me.

You, (other's name), aren't alone — love is all around you.

We, (your name) and (other's name), aren't alone — love is all around us.

(Your name) and (other's name) aren't alone — love is all around them.

When we begin a relationship we often feel generous, open, excited and willing to take risks. Since we don't have much invested, we have little fear of failure. As we grow in commitment to the relationship and see our love returned, it's tempting to hold on tighter, work more, worry more and try to make things go the way we want most.

We don't control our relationships. We may sacrifice the excitement and satisfaction if we try to. We control only our part in the relationship. The other has responsibility for their own part. Our relationships can stay fresh, open and exciting if we remain clear on the limits of our burden in them.

Personal Affirmations

I, (your name), share the burden of a healthy relationship.

You, (your name), share the burden of a healthy relationship.

(Your name) shares the burden of a healthy relationship.

We, (your name) and (other's name), share the burden of a healthy realtionship.

Reciprocal Affirmations

I, (your name), share the burden of our healthy relationship.

You, (other's name), share the burden of our healthy relationship.

We, (your name) and (other's name), share the burden of our healthy relationship.

(Your name) and (other's name) share the burden of their healthy relationship.

Sharing affirmations with another can be a very positive experience. Just sharing our dreams, hopes and aspirations makes them more real, legitimate and likely to happen for us. It also gives the other a greater insight into our goals and the direction of our life.

When listening to another's affirmations, we must remember to listen without judging their wants and goals. When sharing our own affirmations, we need to release any fears of being wrong or appearing stupid or unrealistic. Sharing our affirmations gives us a real vehicle for positive change in our lives.

Personal Affirmations

I, (your name), want to share my affirmations with another.

You, (your name), want to share your affirmations with another.

(Your name) wants to share her/his affirmations with another.

We, (your name) and (other's name), want to share our affirmations with each other.

Reciprocal Affirmations

I, (your name), want to share my affirmations with you.

You, (other's name), want to share your affirmations with me.

We, (your name) and (other's name), want to share our affirmations with each other.

(Your name) and (other's name) want to share their affirmations with each other.

Each of us is different. We have different forces acting upon us. We may respond differently to similar stimuli. For example, some of us respond to stress by eating, some by withdrawing, some by drinking coffee and some by becoming animated. Our different responses are a matter of personal choice.

In a relationship we deal with our own needs and another's at the same time. We may be in different states. For example, one of us may be up and talkative while the other is down and doesn't want to listen. We must avoid subjugating ourselves to another's mood and take care of our own needs while respecting the needs of others.

Personal Affirmations

I, (your name), respect the needs of others.

You, (your name), respect the needs of others.

(Your name) respects the needs of others.

We, (your name) and (other's name), respect the needs of others.

Reciprocal Affirmations

I, (your name), respect your needs.

You, (other's name), respect my needs.

We, (your name) and (other's name), respect each other's needs.

(Your name) and (other's name) respect each other's needs.

Have we ever been cheerfully driving down the road when another driver leaned on the horn, made an obscene gesture and mouthed words that would make anyone blush? How did we respond? Did we get upset, yell back (perhaps with the windows safely closed) and have a rotten day afterward? Or were we able to maintain our good mood and think quietly, "They must have had a bad day."? If we do the latter, we successfully avoid taking on the other's problem.

We experience analogous encounters in our close relationships. We need to be able to walk away from any manipulations and not take on the other's problems.

Personal Affirmations
I, (your name), don't take on another's problems.
You, (your name), don't take on another's problems.
(Your name) doesn't take on another's problems.
We, (your name) and (other's name), don't take on others' problems.

Reciprocal Affirmations
I, (your name), don't take on your problems.
You, (other's name), don't take on my problems.
We, (your name) and (other's name), don't take on each other's problems.
(Your name) and (other's name) don't take on each other's problems.

It's hard to relate to someone with strong body odor or bad breath just because it's unpleasant being close to her/him. Personal hygiene, then, can have a big effect on relationships.

When we consider ourselves important, we spend time bathing, grooming, dressing and taking care of our clothes. The pride that comes from knowing we're clean and neat carries over into the way we feel and act. The combination of feeling good about ourselves and knowing we're not turning others off allows us to relate with confidence.

Personal Affirmations

I, (your name), feel good about my personal hygiene.

You, (your name), feel good about your personal hygiene.

(Your name) feels good about her/his personal hygiene.

We, (your name) and (other's name), feel good about our personal hygiene.

Reciprocal Affirmations

I, (your name), feel good about my personal hygiene.

You, (other's name), feel good about your personal hygiene.

We, (your name) and (other's name), feel good about our personal hygiene.

(Your name) and (other's name) feel good about their personal hygiene.

Every day can be special and exciting with our lover. We don't have to go to a fancy restaurant or nightclub to get that feeling. It can happen in our ordinary day-to-day life.

We need only look at some feature of our relationship that's special and exciting to us. Perhaps it's tenderness, caring, sensuousness or sex. There's something about our lover that can excite us every day. We just have to find it and go after it.

Personal Affirmations

I, (your name), find something exciting about my lover each day.

You, (your name), find something exciting about your lover each day.

(Your name) finds something exciting about her/his lover each day.

We, (your name) and (other's name), find something exciting about each other each day.

Reciprocal Affirmations

I, (your name), find something exciting about you each day.

You, (other's name), find something exciting about me each day.

We, (your name) and (other's name), find something exciting about each other each day.

(Your name) and (other's name) find something exciting about each other each day.

We know that anger is a normal emotion, not one to be hidden or ashamed of. But how do we handle it so our anger isn't destructive to ourselves or others?

The first step in handling anger in a nondestructive way is acknowledging it. "I'm angry. I'm angry!" If we bottle it up, it explodes. We must acknowledge it's there. Second, we must find an acceptable channel to get it out physically, something from pounding the wall or a punching bag to our favorite vigorous exercise.

These steps can help express anger, defuse any destructive elements and result in a positive experience from the emotion of anger.

Personal Affirmations

I, (your name), channel my anger in nondestructive ways.

You, (your name), channel your anger in nondestructive ways.

(Your name) channels her/his anger in nondestructive ways.

We, (your name) and (other's name), each channel our anger in nondestructive ways.

Reciprocal Affirmations

I, (your name), channel my anger in nondestructive ways.

You, (other's name), channel your anger in nondestructive ways.

We, (your name) and (other's name), each channel our anger in nondestructive ways.

(Your name) and (other's name) each channel their anger in nondestructive ways.

Sometimes our partner has deep unresolved pain that comes to the surface whenever there is stress in our relationship. It's not our job to be psychiatrist, analyst or eternally patient listener. Each of us must work through and find release from our own pain. If we feel we must be the perfect listener or pride ourselves on discerning what is really bothering our partner, then we may be enabling our partner to push their pain off onto us instead of healing it themselves.

No matter how supportive we want to be, we're most helpful if we recognize what is our business and what isn't. Be empathetic with the other's painful feelings, but decline the long analysis.

Personal Affirmations

I, (your name), am an empathetic listener without assuming others' pain.

You, (your name), are an empathetic listener without assuming others' pain.

(Your name) is an empathetic listener without assuming others' pain.

We, (your name) and (other's name), are empathetic listeners without assuming others' pain.

Reciprocal Affirmations

I, (your name), listen empathetically without assuming your pain.

You, (other's name), listen empathetically without assuming my pain.

We, (your name) and (other's name), listen empathetically without assuming each other's pain.

(Your name) and (other's name) listen empathetically without assuming each other's pain.

Often we come home from work tired, angry and irritable. We still carry the day's frustrations with us. When we encounter a loved one while we're in this state, we don't radiate love or come across as lovable. This can lead to fights or merely poor communication and can adversely affect our sex life.

We need to leave the frustrations of our workday outside the door of our home and give and receive love freely at home. After all, which is more important, job or family? How many people have said on their death bed, "I wish I'd spent more time at work"?

Personal Affirmations

I, (your name), find and give love at home regardless of my workday.

You, (your name), find and give love at home regardless of your workday.

(Your name) finds and gives love at home regardless of her/his workday.

We, (your name) and (other's name), find and give love at home regardless of our workdays.

Reciprocal Affirmations

I, (your name), find and give love at home regardless of my workday.

You, (other's name), find and give love at home regardless of your workday.

We, (your name) and (other's name), find and give love at home regardless of our workdays.

(Your name) and (other's name) find and give love at home regardless of their workdays.

Sometimes we forget that we are special independent of our relationships to others. Others are essential to the fullness of our lives, to our maximum growth and happiness. But they don't establish, define or control our value.

Today I will examine my relationship with me. Do I appreciate my talents and try to give them opportunities to grow? Do I find small ways to make myself feel good each day with a little pampering? Do I go easier on myself when I'm in a bad mood? Or do I judge myself too harshly, condemn or devalue myself? If I practice having a good relationship with myself, my other relationships will be easier.

Personal Affirmations

I, (your name), go easy on myself and appreciate my talents.

You, (your name), go easy on yourself and appreciate your talents.

(Your name) goes easy on herself/himself and appreciates her/his talents.

We, (your name) and (other's name), go easy on ourselves and appreciate our talents.

Reciprocal Affirmations

I, (your name), go easy on myself and appreciate my talents.

You, (other's name), go easy on yourself and appreciate your talents.

We, (your name) and (other's name), go easy on ourselves and appreciate our talents.

(Your name) and (other's name) go easy on themselves and appreciate their talents.

Spring is the time of year nature renews itself. Flowers and trees blossom forth from winter dormancy. Wild animals give birth and nurture their young. We rake our gardens to rid them of dead plant material from last year, and we spring-clean our homes to rid them of the past's unwanted dirt and possessions.

We can learn from nature. As the days get longer, we feel renewed energy. We can use some of that energy to renew and nurture our relationships. Perhaps in our winter doldrums we haven't given our relationships as much attention as we wish we had. Now is the time to get rid of the past's unwanted habits and help our relationships blossom anew.

Personal Affirmations

I, (your name), put renewed energy into my relationships.

You, (your name), put renewed energy into your relationships.

(Your name) puts renewed energy into her/his relationships.

We, (your name) and (other's name), put renewed energy into our relationships.

Reciprocal Affirmations

I, (your name), put renewed energy into our relationship.

You, (other's name), put renewed energy into our relationship.

We, (your name) and (other's name), put renewed energy into our relationship.

(Your name) and (other's name) put renewed energy into their relationship.

Which decisions should be joint and which should be individual? Individual decisions are appropriate when only the decison-maker has to act or not act, such as choosing what job to take or whether to play tennis with friends.

Joint decisions are appropriate when both people are required to act, such as choosing where to live, where to take a joint vacation or what livingroom furniture to buy.

Before we make a joint decision, we need to ask ourselves whether it needs joint input or whether it is really the province of one of us alone.

Personal Affirmations

I, (your name), make joint decisions only when appro-
    priate.
You, (your name), make joint decisions only when
    appropriate.
(Your name) makes joint decisions only when appro-
    priate.
We, (your name) and (other's name), make joint deci-
    sions only when appropriate.

Reciprocal Affirmations

I, (your name), make joint decisions only when appro-
    priate.
You, (other's name), make joint decisions only when
    appropriate.
We, (your name) and (other's name), make joint deci-
    sions only when appropriate.
(Your name) and (other's name) make joint decisions
    only when appropriate.

When we're in a troubling situation, which do we do first — look for a solution or look for someone to blame for getting us into the situation? From a practical point of view, solving our current problem by finding a solution is all that matters. From a relationship point of view, the same holds true.

Our relationship isn't served by recriminations. Laying blame only creates an additional problem, one in our relationship. It doesn't solve our current problem. Since we can't change others anyway, blaming them is futile. We need to concentrate on the here and now and on solutions.

Personal Affirmations
I, (your name), find solutions, not scapegoats.
You, (your name), find solutions, not scapegoats.
(Your name) finds solutions, not scapegoats.
We, (your name) and (other's name), find solutions,
not scapegoats.

Reciprocal Affirmations
I, (your name), find solutions, not scapegoats.
You, (other's name), find solutions, not scapegoats.
We, (your name) and (other's name), find solutions,
not scapegoats.
(Your name) and (other's name) find solutions, not
scapegoats.

We have the ability to increase our confidence in our relationships without waiting for change in others. Our confidence gets robbed by guilt, worry, anxiety and fear. Guilt is really fear of the past. We fear that something in our past will darken our lives. Worry is fear of the future. The risks of living feel overwhelming. Anxiety is fear of the present. We feel insecure because we doubt ourselves or the people or situation around us.

We can let go of our fears by focusing only on the present, this day or this hour. I can make the best of the present without fear.

Personal Affirmations
I, (your name), focus on the present with confidence.
You, (your name), focus on the present with confidence.
(Your name) focuses on the present with confidence.
We, (your name) and (other's name), focus on the present with confidence.

Reciprocal Affirmations
I, (your name), focus on the present with confidence.
You, (other's name), focus on the present with confidence.
We, (your name) and (other's name), focus on the present with confidence.
(Your name) and (other's name) focus on the present with confidence.

Our relationships are in a process of constant growth. If we are stagnating in a relationship, like the earth in winter, we can welcome new opportunities for spring. Fear of change causes more trouble than change itself. We can trust that challenges to a relationship stimulate its growth.

If we fear change in ourselves or the other, we limit the growth of our relationship and create anxiety and tension. As the earth renews itself in this spring season, I will welcome the new changes and challenges that stretch and stimulate me and my relationships.

Personal Affirmations

I, (your name), welcome growth with calm confidence.

You, (your name), welcome growth with calm confidence.

(Your name) welcomes growth with calm confidence.

We, (your name) and (other's name), welcome growth with calm confidence.

Reciprocal Affirmations

I, (your name), welcome your growth with calm confidence.

You, (other's name), welcome my growth with calm confidence.

We, (your name) and (other's name), welcome each other's growth with calm confidence.

(Your name) and (other's name) welcome each other's growth with calm confidence.

No matter what we do or have done, what we look like or what thoughts we have or have had, we each deserve unconditional love. Yet we will not receive them unless we accept that we deserve them. If we are suspicious of gifts, attention or expressions of love, we cannot enjoy them. If we discount them because of painful secrets and fear of unworthiness, then they can turn sour or seem empty to us.

We can nurture openness, gratitude and acceptance of love and affection. They are always earned rewards for being ourselves. Rather than increasing our psychic indebtedness, they affirm our worthiness just as we are now.

Personal Affirmations

I, (your name), feel deserving of love and affection.

You, (your name), feel deserving of love and affection.

(Your name) feels deserving of love and affection.

We, (your name) and (other's name), feel deserving of love and affection.

Reciprocal Affirmations

I, (your name), feel deserving of your love and affection.

You, (other's name), feel deserving of my love and affection.

We, (your name) and (other's name), deserve each other's love and affection.

(Your name) and (other's name) deserve each other's love and affection.

The media have led us to seek instant gratification of our wants. But change or progress in our lives or relationships often happens slowly. It can be hard to accept that many important things take time.

If we see positive progress in our relationships, we need to allow time to nurture that progress. We need patience with ourselves and with others. Steady progress will, over time, result in a big change. Patience helps us see small changes through to the end result of a happier life or better relationship.

Personal Affirmations
I, (your name), patiently accept small steady gains.
You, (your name), patiently accept small steady gains.
(Your name) patiently accepts small steady gains.
We, (your name) and (other's name), patiently accept small steady gains.

Reciprocal Affirmations
I, (your name), patiently accept small steady gains.
You, (other's name), patiently accept small steady gains.
We, (your name) and (other's name), patiently accept small steady gains.
(Your name) and (other's name) patiently accept small steady gains.

If we have trouble in relationships, we may blame it on qualities in ourselves that we believe are less than perfect and yet impossible to change. We wish we were more beautiful, smarter, wealthier, more generous, more confident, more mature or more youthful. We feel frustrated that we cannot change these things. We may even wrestle with them unsuccessfully.

But all these things can change for the better if we nurture our good qualities and stop focusing on the bad. Each of us has good and beauty within. If we spend our time and energy on these, they will manifest on the outside, improving our attractiveness and our behavior toward others.

Personal Affirmations

I, (your name), nurture my good qualities to over-
    shadow my faults.

You, (your name), nurture your good qualities to over-
    shadow your faults.

(Your name) nurtures her/his good qualities to over-
    shadow her/his faults.

We, (your name) and (other's name), nurture our
    good qualities to overshadow our faults.

Reciprocal Affirmations

I, (your name), nurture my good qualities to over-
    shadow my faults.

You, (other's name), nurture your good qualities to
    overshadow your faults.

We, (your name) and (other's name), nurture our
    good qualities to overshadow our faults.

(Your name) and (other's name) nurture their good
    qualities to overshadow their faults.

We've all felt we've handled a situation with someone else poorly. Many of us have felt guilty or even embarrassed that we made fools of ourselves. The good news is that we always get a second chance. We're very likely to see the person again and have the opportunity to behave the way we wish we had the first time. Even if we don't we've learned to deal more kindly with others.

We needn't get bogged down in worry or guilt over the encounter we feel went poorly. We can identify what we think we did badly and how we would like to do it the next time. Then we can get ready for that second chance.

Personal Affirmations

I, (your name), always have another chance to do things better.

You, (your name), always have another chance to do things better.

(Your name) always has another chance to do things better.

We, (your name) and (other's name), always have another chance to do things better.

Reciprocal Affirmations

I, (your name), always have another chance to do things better.

You, (other's name), always have another chance to do things better.

We, (your name) and (other's name), always have another chance to do things better.

(Your name) and (other's name) always have another chance to do things better.

No matter how good, bad or indifferent a relationship is, it won't stay the same. Like the universe, relationships aren't static. Relationships take work and time. If we don't see someone, we grow apart and can rarely pick up where we left off for more than a few hours because we just don't have the closeness we once had.

We have a choice with each relationship. There's no harm in letting a relationship die and moving on. But if we want to continue a good relationship or improve one, it takes time and attention.

Personal Affirmations

I, (your name), attend to the relationships I want to continue.

You, (your name), attend to the relationships you want to continue.

(Your name) attends to the relationships she/he wants to continue.

We, (your name) and (other's name), attend to the relationships we want to continue.

Reciprocal Affirmations

I, (your name), attend to our relationship.

You, (other's name), attend to our relationship.

We, (your name) and (other's name), attend to our relationship.

(Your name) and (other's name) attend to their relationship.

We would do well to let some silliness into our lives. People who play and laugh together add a dimension to their relationship. Chatting with a pet, putting on a silly hat or costume, skipping instead of walking, inventing limericks, finding a far-fetched pun — anything that is free of purpose, planning and pain gives us a release. It helps us break out of straight-line thinking, emotion-filled mind traps and narrowed perspectives.

Sharing silliness with others can make us feel vulnerable. Perhaps our parents told us, "Don't be silly," so we feel naughty when we do it. And no one wants to be laughed at. But the possibility of having someone laugh with us is worth the risk.

Personal Affirmations
I, (your name), am not afraid to be silly.
You, (your name), aren't afraid to be silly.
(Your name) isn't afraid to be silly.
We, (your name) and (other's name), aren't afraid to be silly.

Reciprocal Affirmations
I, (your name), am not afraid to be silly.
You, (other's name), aren't afraid to be silly.
We, (your name) and (other's name), aren't afraid to be silly.
(Your name) and (other's name) aren't afraid to be silly.

When we tell others what to do, we are invading their space. This is true even if they don't object. Our advice, seen from our perspective, looks right to us, but we can have no way of knowing if it's right from the other's perspective. We don't walk in the other's shoes.

We have no business invading another's space. They need the space to make their own decisions, make their own mistakes (although we aren't in a position to judge if they are mistakes) and to have their own successes. It's through this process that people gain the confidence and self-esteem to independently make better decisions next time.

Personal Affirmations

I, (your name), leave others space to make their own decisions.

You, (your name), leave others space to make their own decisions.

(Your name) leaves others space to make their own decisions.

We, (your name) and (other's name), leave others space to make their own decisions.

Reciprocal Affirmations

I, (your name), leave you space to make your own decisions.

You, (other's name), leave me space to make my own decisions.

We, (your name) and (other's name), leave each other space to make our own decisions.

(Your name) and (other's name) leave each other space to make their own decisions.

In an achievement-oriented society, we're often encouraged to push ourselves beyond our comfort zone. This enlivens us and helps us grow. But there is another level we must consider. If we push ourselves too far, we are liable to fall into a trap of expecting something in return.

We need to think clearly about our comfort zone of acceptable risk. If we go further than that we begin to expect and rely on predictable responses from others in order to justify pushing ourselves so far. We deny their right to respond in new ways by having our comfort depend on their predictability. Instead, we need to push ourselves only as far as is comfortable.

Personal Affirmations

I, (your name), don't rely on others' reactions for my comfort.

You, (your name), don't rely on others' reactions for your comfort.

(Your name) doesn't rely on others' reactions for her/his comfort.

We, (your name) and (other's name), don't rely on others' reactions for our comfort.

Reciprocal Affirmations

I, (your name), don't rely on your reactions for my comfort.

You, (other's name), don't rely on my reactions for your comfort.

We, (your name) and (other's name), don't rely on each other's reactions for our comfort.

(Your name) and (other's name) don't rely on each other's reactions for their comfort.

Each of us has one of two basic attitudes toward life: positive or negative. Some express this as optimistic or pessimistic, or seeing the cup half full or half empty. The attitude we bring to all our experiences is in our minds. We have control over it.

A positive attitude allows us to look forward to the day, to see the bright side of things, to have hope and patience and to allow good things to happen to us. A positive attitude allows us to smile at others, joke around and be cheerful. It gives us strength to go through difficult times.

Personal Affirmations

I, (your name), choose a positive attitude toward life.

You, (your name), choose a positive attitude toward life.

(Your name) chooses a positive attitude toward life.

We, (your name) and (other's name), choose a positive attitude toward life.

Reciprocal Affirmations

I, (your name), choose a positive attitude toward life.

You, (other's name), choose a positive attitude toward life.

We, (your name) and (other's name), choose a positive attitude toward life.

(Your name) and (other's name) choose a positive attitude toward life.

It's easy to get into habits of negative thinking and speaking about those close to us. But negative characterizations only tie them to their past and discourage them from positive change. If we believe our partner is careless or thoughtless, for example, our judgments, accusations or "helpful suggestions" will only help keep them so.

Subtle changes in how we think and speak can introduce more positive habits. If we say, "That was sure thoughtless!" we are accusing and labeling. The other may feel defensive and angry. If instead we say, "I am put off by the way you handled that," we are expressing our own feelings, avoiding labels and acknowledging the other's freedom to choose their actions.

Personal Affirmations

I, (your name), avoid labeling others and free them to grow.

You, (your name), avoid labeling others and free them to grow.

(Your name) avoids labeling others and frees them to grow.

We, (your name) and (other's name), avoid labeling others and free them to grow.

Reciprocal Affirmations

I, (your name), avoid labeling you and free you to grow.

You, (other's name), avoid labeling me and free me to grow.

We, (your name) and (other's name), avoid labeling each other and free each other to grow.

(Your name) and (other's name) avoid labeling each other and free each other to grow.

Sometimes a fear of growing older puts strain on our relationships. The realization that we are aging highlights any gap between our personal goals and our present condition. We may be in a relationship that doesn't match our ideal. Or we hope for changes within our relationship that seem too slow in coming.

The strain of wishing things were different has two effects. First, we may let go of our ideals and goals, deciding we are already over the hill. Second, we may adopt a sense of urgency, insisting on change for the sake of change. We can look forward to our tomorrows if we accept that living today as best we can will bring a better tomorrow.

Personal Affirmations
I, (your name), believe in my future.
You, (your name), believe in your future.
(Your name) believes in her/his future.
We, (your name) and (other's name), believe in our future.

Reciprocal Affirmations
I, (your name), believe in your future.
You, (other's name), believe in my future.
We, (your name) and (other's name), believe in our future.
(Your name) and (other's name) believe in their future.

Sometimes we feel stuck in a relationship. If it's a romantic relationship, we may remember the feelings we used to have, such as that the other person was the "right" one for us. In many ways, society encourages us to stick with a bad relationship. Examples are the marriage vow, "Till death do us part," staying together "for the sake of the kids," and society's judgment that the only successful relationship is a long-term one. We're reluctant to admit that we've changed or that we could have made a mistake.

Each day I choose, consciously or unconsciously, to stay in a relationship or get out of it and to keep it the same or change it. Each day the choice is mine.

Personal Affirmations

I, (your name), have choices in each of my relationships.

You, (your name), have choices in each of your relationships.

(Your name) has choices in each of her/his relationships.

We, (your name) and (other's name), have choices in each of our relationships.

Reciprocal Affirmations

I, (your name), have choices in our relationship.

You, (other's name), have choices in our relationship.

We, (your name) and (other's name), each have choices in our relationship.

(Your name) and (other's name) each have choices in their relationship.

We've been taught and may have found it helpful to be cynical and distrustful of others in today's complex world. While that may be good advice as applied to politicians, advertising hype and telemarketing sales-people, it really hinders many relationships.

We have a number of different types of relationships in our lives: casual but regular relationships with the newsstand person, clerks at stores we frequent and people at gas stations and lunch spots; professional relationships with our bosses, co-workers and subordinates; and close relationships with our friends and family. We need to be open to an appropriate level of trust for each relationship.

Personal Affirmations

I, (your name), trust others appropriately.
You, (your name), trust others appropriately.
(Your name) trusts others appropriately.
We, (your name) and (other's name), trust others appropriately.

Reciprocal Affirmations

I, (your name), trust you appropriately.
You, (other's name), trust me appropriately.
We, (your name) and (other's name), trust each other appropriately.
(Your name) and (other's name) trust each other appropriately.

Bad experiences can make us wary of people. How can we restore our faith in people? Is it a choice between wariness and freely handing over our life savings or opening our hearts at the drop of a hat?

We need to distinguish between our feelings toward others and our feelings toward ourselves. If we push ourselves to trust others but don't trust ourselves, we're likely to end up betrayed, victimized or taken advantage of. But if we like ourselves, trust our intuition about how far to go in a relationship and pay attention to the boundaries of our comfort zone, we move comfortably among others and grow to like them more and more.

Personal Affirmations

I, (your name), grow to like myself and others more and more.

You, (your name), grow to like yourself and others more and more.

(Your name) grows to like herself/himself and others more and more.

We, (your name) and (other's name), grow to like ourselves and others more and more.

Reciprocal Affirmations

I, (your name), grow to like myself and you more and more.

You, (other's name), grow to like yourself and me more and more.

We, (your name) and (other's name), grow to like ourselves and each other more and more.

(Your name) and (other's name) grow to like themselves and each other more and more.

There are many chores associated with running a modern household, such as meal preparation, meal cleanup, laundry, cleaning, shopping, child care, earning money, paying the bills, lawn care and household repairs. How we divide up these chores helps define our relationship. Do we have a cooperative, sharing relationship, a master/servant relationship or something in between?

Our deepest relationships need cooperation and sharing. We shouldn't assume, for example, that men are responsible for providing money and women for other chores. If such roles don't feel comfortable to either partner or if they feel uneven in responsibility or time requirements, they must be talked about and altered. We each need to be comfortable with our part.

Personal Affirmations
I, (your name), deserve to be comfortable with my chores.
You, (your name), deserve to be comfortable with your chores.
(Your name) deserves to be comfortable with her/his chores.
We, (your name) and (other's name), each deserve to be comfortable with our chores.

Reciprocal Affirmations
I, (your name), deserve to be comfortable with my chores.
You, (other's name), deserve to be comfortable with your chores.
We, (your name) and (other's name), each deserve to be comfortable with our chores.
(Your name) and (other's name) each deserve to be comfortable with their chores.

When we are dividing chores in our household relationships, it's helpful to consider whether our preferences depend on role models, natural inclinations or social judgments. A man may like to cook, for example, but be uncomfortable taking on cooking as his responsibility because of conventional divisions of chores. A woman may choose to do home repairs around the house in rebellion against her mother's dependence on her father for all home repairs.

It's not for one of us to judge the other's motives. But if we know our own motives and reveal them to the other, we can more easily negotiate the most comfortable mix of chores and feel free to seek a revision when motives change.

Personal Affirmations

I, (your name), have my own motives and respect those of others.

You, (your name), have your own motives and respect those of others.

(Your name) has her/his own motives and respects those of others.

We, (your name) and (other's name), each have our own motives and respect those of others.

Reciprocal Affirmations

I, (your name), have my own motives and I respect your motives.

You, (other's name), have your own motives and you respect mine.

We, (your name) and (other's name), respect each other's motives.

(Your name) and (other's name) respect each other's motives.

"What a gorgeous spring day!" We feel great on days like that, and it feels great to be able to share them with another. It feels good to have that connection of sharing the beauty of nature and the universe with another.

The same good feelings go with sharing a beautiful sunset, frost on the leaves, a placid lake, crashing ocean waves, a starlit night or a beautiful mountain scene. Sharing our connection to nature with another builds our relationship.

Personal Affirmations
I, (your name), share the wonders of nature with others.
You, (your name), share the wonders of nature with others.
(Your name) shares the wonders of nature with others.
We, (your name) and (other's name), share the wonders of nature with others.

Reciprocal Affirmations
I, (your name), share the wonders of nature with you.
You, (other's name), share the wonders of nature with me.
We, (your name) and (other's name), share the wonders of nature with each other.
(Your name) and (other's name) share the wonders of nature with each other.

The people with whom we spend our time can influence our moods and attitudes. Job, extended family or organizational commitments may leave us little chance to choose with whom we spend our time. Or we may feel we have no real choice because we can't tell until later how they affect us.

But how we feel when we are with them is the best touchstone. If they complain and criticize frequently about others, us or even the weather, their negative attitude will wear us down quickly. In contrast, if they praise and enjoy, they will bolster our spirits. It's worth seeking out positive people, even if we only see them once a month.

Personal Affirmations

I, (your name), seek out people who praise rather than complain.

You, (your name), seek out people who praise rather than complain.

(Your name) seeks out people who praise rather than complain.

We, (your name) and (other's name), seek out people who praise rather than complain.

Reciprocal Affirmations

I, (your name), prefer it when you praise rather than complain.

You, (other's name), prefer it when I praise rather than complain.

We, (your name) and (other's name), prefer it when we praise rather than complain.

(Your name) and (other's name) prefer it when they praise rather than complain.

We've all noticed that some people always seem cheerful or happy, while others always complain or seem depressed. Some of the cheerful people have circumstances or problems that are every bit as bad as or worse than the depressed people. Why?

Attitude doesn't reflect circumstances or the number or degree of problems in one's life. Attitude reflects our outlook on life, how we feel about ourselves, and how we choose to perceive the universe. We have control over our outlook. We can take a more cheerful view of life.

Personal Affirmations

I, (your name), look at things cheerfully.
You, (your name), look at things cheerfully.
(Your name) looks at things cheerfully.
We, (your name) and (other's name), look at things cheerfully.

Reciprocal Affirmations

I, (your name), look at things cheerfully.
You, (other's name), look at things cheerfully.
We, (your name) and (other's name), look at things cheerfully.
(Your name) and (other's name) look at things cheerfully.

Sometimes the laudable practice of cooperation is used as a tool for manipulation. Cooperative decisions turn into veto struggles. Or one person "cooperates" by helping the other with chores, only to find no reciprocal help and a double burden. We must be careful not to ignore our own needs under the guise of cooperation.

Cooperation is a sharing of duties and responsibilities in order to achieve some common purpose. A giving spirit on all sides is important. A cooperative spirit will lead to spontaneous cooperative assistance without expectation of return. The good feelings from generous cooperation tend to infect all concerned.

Personal Affirmations
I, (your name), cooperate without manipulation.
You, (your name), cooperate without manipulation.
(Your name) cooperates without manipulation.
We, (your name) and (other's name), cooperate without manipulation.

Reciprocal Affirmations
I, (your name), cooperate with you without manipulating you.
You, (other's name), cooperate with me without manipulating me.
We, (your name) and (other's name), cooperate with each other without manipulating.
(Your name) and (other's name) cooperate with each other without manipulation.

Bliss or extreme joy is our natural state of being. Due to the upsets of modern life, many of us are off the natural track and trying to get back to the bliss we experienced in the womb and perhaps in the early years of our lives.

Our principal love relationship is naturally blissful. Here too, the stresses and strains of daily life take their toll and make it hard for us to experience bliss consistently. But like anything else, if we're aware of our goal of bliss in our relationship, believe in it, desire it, are committed to it and are persistent, we will experience more and more bliss.

Personal Affirmations
I, (your name), find bliss in my relationship.
You, (your name), find bliss in your relationship.
(Your name) finds bliss in her/his relationship.
We, (your name) and (other's name), find bliss in our relationship.

Reciprocal Affirmations
I, (your name), find bliss in our relationship.
You, (other's name), find bliss in our relationship.
We, (your name) and (other's name), find bliss in our relationship.
(Your name) and (other's name) find bliss in their relationship.

Controlling our attitude or outlook on life is easier than it sounds. To have a better attitude or more cheerful outlook, we need only look for the good in every situation, the bright side of things.

Nearly every situation, no matter how bleak, has some nugget of good in it, some element of humor which can cheer us. We're on this planet for the duration of our lives, so we might as well enjoy it. I will concentrate on the bright side today.

Personal Affirmations

I, (your name), find the good in every situation.
You, (your name), find the good in every situation.
(Your name) finds the good in every situation.
We, (your name) and (other's name), find the good in every situation.

Reciprocal Affirmations

I, (your name), find the good in every situation.
You, (other's name), find the good in every situation.
We, (your name) and (other's name), find the good in every situation.
(Your name) and (other's name) find the good in every situation.

Jealousy can be, as Shakespeare said, a monster. Even if we aren't consumed with sexual jealousy, little jealousies may sabotage our attempts to develop better relationships. Do I feel jealous of my companion's time spent with others? Of their reading instead of talking to me? Of their easy-going style with children that switches to uncomfortable seriousness around me?

Jealousy is a form of dependence. We project onto another our deepest fears of our own unlovableness. We believe that their manifest devotion is essential to our happiness. But if we decide when, where and how another is to love us, we prevent them from being and expressing themselves. We make it harder for them to love us.

Personal Affirmations

I, (your name), let go of little jealousies.

You, (your name), let go of little jealousies.

(Your name) lets go of little jealousies.

We, (your name) and (other's name), let go of little jealousies.

Reciprocal Affirmations

I, (your name), let go of little jealousies.

You, (other's name), let go of little jealousies.

We, (your name) and (other's name), let go of little jealousies.

(Your name) and (other's name) let go of little jealousies.

We need to let go of any thought of changing another person. Each has their own path and choices to make. We cannot make another person adjust to our desires. But we are far from helpless to affect them in a positive way and to bring out the best in them. This we do by nurturing our faith that if we model loving, rational, happy thought and behavior, the other will tend in that direction too.

A resonance and shared vibration connects us all. If I act, speak and smile in ways that make me feel good, the effect on others will be more than I imagine.

Personal Affirmations

I, (your name), help others by looking to my own attitude.

You, (your name), help others by looking to your own attitude.

(Your name) helps others by looking to her/his own attitude.

We, (your name) and (other's name), help others by looking to our own attitudes.

Reciprocal Affirmations

I, (your name), help you by looking to my own attitude.

You, (other's name), help me by looking to your own attitude.

We, (your name) and (other's name), help each other by looking to our own attitudes.

(Your name) and (other's name) help each other by looking to their own attitudes.

When we have a problem with a relationship, do we solicit advice from our sister, mother, best friends or co-workers? Do we add up the votes on the advice before we make a decision? Do we then still feel confused and unsure of what to do?

When we act from our own internal feelings, not from external advice, our actions are more likely to be comfortable and right for us. Taking a poll doesn't help. Seeking empathy and listening for options, not advice, does.

Personal Affirmations

I, (your name), ask for empathy and options, not advice.

You, (your name), ask for empathy and options, not advice.

(Your name) asks for empathy and options, not advice.

We, (your name) and (other's name), ask for empathy and options, not advice.

Reciprocal Affirmations

I, (your name), ask you for empathy and options, not advice.

You, (other's name), ask me for empathy and options, not advice.

We, (your name) and (other's name), ask each other for empathy and options, not advice.

(Your name) and (other's name) ask each other for empathy and options, not advice.

As we get older, we may find birthdays uncomfortable. We assume that birthday celebrations are for kids eager to become adults, and that once we become adults, birthdays are nasty reminders that we are aging.

But just as a healthy child enjoys each year of childhood, we can appreciate each year in its fullness and uniqueness. We will have little regret for a birthday if we have lived the year to the best of our ability.

Each birthday is a chance to take stock, to be grateful for benefits that we've had, to let go of hardships, to appreciate the growth we've experienced in our relationships and to share our satisfactions with someone else.

Personal Affirmations

I, (your name), make the most of my birthday.
You, (your name), make the most of your birthday.
(Your name) makes the most of her/his birthday.
We, (your name) and (other's name), make the most of our birthdays.

Reciprocal Affirmations

I, (your name), make the most of my birthday.
You, (other's name), make the most of your birthday.
We, (your name) and (other's name), make the most of our birthdays.
(Your name) and (other's name) make the most of their birthdays.

When we share deeply-held value systems with another, we find it easy to relate to them. We understand the other's basic philosophy of life.

When we want to establish or maintain a relationship, exploring our values or philosophy of life together can help us get to know each other. It's very affirming to feel that the other understands us. If we work on building a common value system, we are likely to draw closer together and build a stronger relationship.

Personal Affirmations

I, (your name), build a common value system with those close.

You, (your name), build a common value system with those close.

(Your name) builds a common value system with those close.

We, (your name) and (other's name), build a common value system with those close.

Reciprocal Affirmations

I, (your name), build a common value system with you.

You, (other's name), build a common value system with me.

We, (your name) and (other's name), build a common value system together.

(Your name) and (other's name) build a common value system together.

At times we keep score of supposed wrongs that someone has done to us. We nurture self-pity while we avoid confrontation and let resentments build. But at any time these accumulated resentments can cause an outburst when we don't even know why. They can exaggerate our next reaction when we think we've had the last straw. They can cause distance between us so there are fewer opportunities to build positive interactions.

When we feel wronged, we need to express our feelings promptly with a minimum of blame and accusation or else let them go entirely with forgiveness and compassion.

Personal Affirmations

I, (your name), don't harbor resentments from the past.

You, (your name), don't harbor resentments from the past.

(Your name) doesn't harbor resentments from the past.

We, (your name) and (other's name), don't harbor resentments from the past.

Reciprocal Affirmations

I, (your name), don't harbor resentments about you from the past.

You, (other's name), don't harbor resentments about me from the past.

We, (your name) and (other's name), don't harbor resentments about each other from the past.

(Your name) and (other's name) don't harbor resentments about each other from the past.

Many of us have a great fear of making a fool of ourselves or looking silly, especially in front of someone close like a parent, child, lover or friend. We need to acknowledge that everyone can and does make mistakes. We all do things that, if judged by a Supreme Being, would be seen as foolish or wrong. We are, after all, only human.

We need to realize that, if we or another person are judging us, we or they shouldn't be. And we need to disregard the fear of those judgments and feel free to be human.

Personal Affirmations

I, (your name), am free of the fear of looking foolish.

You, (your name), are free of the fear of looking foolish.

(Your name) is free of the fear of looking foolish.

We, (your name) and (other's name), are free of the fear of looking foolish.

Reciprocal Affirmations

I, (your name), am free of the fear of looking foolish to you.

You, (other's name), are free of the fear of looking foolish to me.

We, (your name) and (other's name), are free of the fear of looking foolish to each other.

(Your name) and (other's name) are free of the fear of looking foolish to each other.

When we plan a celebration in a relationship, we need to make it meaningful and fun for both. If it's too big, too much work or lacks symbolism for one of us, we miss the rewards of celebration — the pleasure, the opportunity to congratulate ourselves and feel proud and grateful, the chance to enjoy the fruits of our good relationship.

When I design a celebration, I will not demand or expect equal enthusiasm for all aspects but will share the planning. Small events may be as meaningful as big ones — like looking at old photos, calling friends who were involved or going for a walk in the park.

Personal Affirmations

I, (your name), design celebrations that are fun and meaningful.

You, (your name), design celebrations that are fun and meaningful.

(Your name) designs celebrations that are fun and meaningful.

We, (your name) and (other's name), design celebrations that are fun and meaningful.

Reciprocal Affirmations

I, (your name), design celebrations that are fun and meaningful.

You, (other's name), design celebrations that are fun and meaningful.

We, (your name) and (other's name), design celebrations that are fun and meaningful.

(Your name) and (other's name) design celebrations that are fun and meaningful.

We all have dreams, hopes and aspirations. Some of them seem so far-fetched that we won't talk about them for fear others will think us unrealistic or just plain silly. A fantasy such as, "I wish I were the Queen or King of England," is impossible. But dreams of owning our own business, being a best-selling author or buying a house are possible.

Sharing our dreams with another helps get them out of the fantasy category and into the "can do" category. It improves our relationship by showing our trust in the other as we reveal something personal and let the other get to know us better.

Personal Affirmations

I, (your name), share my dreams with others.

You, (your name), share your dreams with others.

(Your name) shares her/his dreams with others.

We, (your name) and (other's name), share our dreams with others.

Reciprocal Affirmations

I, (your name), share my dreams with you.

You, (other's name), share your dreams with me.

We, (your name) and (other's name), share our dreams with each other.

(Your name) and (other's name) share their dreams with each other.

Our moods affect the way we feel and interact. The way we interact affects our relationship. If we are in a bad mood, we may be sullen, nasty or uncommunicative. This can lead to harsh words and a fight. Maybe it's a rainy, dreary day. Maybe our body cycles are affecting us. Maybe we just ate a sweet pastry and got a shock of sugar.

If we realize many moods are brought on by the weather, biorhythms or what we've eaten or haven't eaten, we can adjust. We can realize our mood isn't brought on by the other and we can avoid taking it out on them.

Personal Affirmations

I, (your name), don't take it out on another when I'm in a bad mood.

You, (your name), don't take it out on another when you're in a bad mood.

(Your name) doesn't take it out on another when she/he is in a bad mood.

We, (your name) and (other's name), don't take it out on others when we're in a bad mood.

Reciprocal Affirmations

I, (your name), don't take it out on you when I'm in a bad mood.

You, (other's name), don't take it out on me when you're in a bad mood.

We, (your name) and (other's name), don't take it out on each other when we're in a bad mood.

(Your name) and (other's name) don't take it out on each other when they're in a bad mood.

Some of us wish we had a friend of the same sex with whom we could share more than sports, cars, electronic gadgets, cosmetics, recipes or clothes and dating stories. Yet we are afraid to open up about our hopes, fears and aspirations, to express our deep feelings. If a man, we fear losing our macho image and perhaps being thought weird. If a woman, we fear cattiness and perhaps being thought a basket case.

Overcoming our fears is a gradual process of building trust between two people.

Personal Affirmations

I, (your name), take the first step in building a friendship.

You, (your name), take the first step in building a friendship.

(Your name) takes the first step in building a friendship.

We, (your name) and (other's name), take the first step in building friendships.

Reciprocal Affirmations

I, (your name), take the first step in building a friendship.

You, (other's name), take the first step in building a friendship.

We, (your name) and (other's name), take the first step in building friendships.

(Your name) and (other's name) take the first step in building friendships.

Sometimes we confuse sacrifice with sharing. We sacrifice when we disregard our own feelings in favor of another's desires or give up something so someone else can have it. Sacrifice comes from a feeling of scarcity, either/or, "we can't have it." We must be careful not to feel we have given up something we want or sacrificed it for someone else. The feelings of sacrifice or martyrdom are detrimental to us and our relationship.

We share when we willingly give. We feel better when we share something of ourselves. Sharing comes from a feeling of abundance, that there is enough for all and "we can both have it." The difference is one of attitude.

Personal Affirmations
I, (your name), share without sacrifice.
You, (your name), share without sacrifice.
(Your name) shares without sacrifice.
We, (your name) and (other's name), share without sacrifice.

Reciprocal Affirmations
I, (your name), share without sacrifice.
You, (other's name), share without sacrifice.
We, (your name) and (other's name), share without sacrifice.
(Your name) and (other's name) share without sacrifice.

If we find ourselves struggling to create a positive attitude, we need to note that struggle is a behavior more likely to keep us negative. We will be better able to project a positive attitude if we act in positive ways. If we behave in ways that signify a positive state of affairs, our attitude will respond and problems will tend toward positive resolution.

If we add a bounce to our step, smile or nod at others, mumble compassionate or friendly words rather than bitter ones, our mood and attitude will improve. Just as the mind has healing power over the body, so the body can heal the mind.

Personal Affirmations

I, (your name), build a positive mood with the things I do.

You, (your name), build a positive mood with the things you do.

(Your name) builds a positive mood with the things she/he does.

We, (your name) and (other's name), build positive moods with the things we do.

Reciprocal Affirmations

I, (your name), build a positive mood with the things I do.

You, (other's name), build a positive mood with the things you do.

We, (your name) and (other's name), build positive moods with the things we do.

(Your name) and (other's name) build positive moods with the things they do.

When we want to share positive feelings it may not be enough to say "I feel good" or "I feel happy." We will find greater satisfaction if we have cultivated a rich vocabulary of positive feeling words that express our mood exactly, such as serene, content, joyful, playful, cozy, ecstatic, cosmic, lusty, satisfied, and so on.

When we make the effort to identify our feelings, we will not only appreciate and enjoy them more ourselves but we will express them more clearly to others. Others will then be better equipped to respond in an understanding and appropriate way that will add to our positive feelings.

Personal Affirmations
I, (your name), use my positive feeling vocabulary.
You, (your name), use your positive feeling vocabulary.
(Your name), uses her/his positive feeling vocabulary.
We, (your name) and (other's name), use our positive feeling vocabularies.

Reciprocal Affirmations
I, (your name), use my positive feeling vocabulary.
You, (other's name), use your positive feeling vocabulary.
We, (your name) and (other's name), use our positive feeling vocabularies.
(Your name) and (other's name) use their positive feeling vocabularies.

The happy times are the best times of our lives. What is happiness? It's an emotional response we have to people or events. How do we get it? Consciously or unconsciously, we choose to have a positive, joyful emotional response to what's going on around us.

Have we noticed that two people in similar circumstances may react differently to the same news, one positive and happy and the other negative, complaining and miserable? We can choose an attitude of joy and happiness toward our lives.

Personal Affirmations

Today I, (your name), choose to see the joyful side of things.

Today you, (your name), choose to see the joyful side of things.

Today (your name) chooses to see the joyful side of things.

Today we, (your name) and (other's name), choose to see the joyful side of things.

Reciprocal Affirmations

Today I, (your name), choose to see the joyful side of things.

Today you, (other's name), choose to see the joyful side of things.

Today we, (your name) and (other's name), choose to see the joyful side of things.

Today (your name) and (other's name) choose to see the joyful side of things.

In a long-term relationship we may feel stuck in a pattern. We may wish things were different but not believe they can change or know how to change them. Often we unknowingly get satisfaction or security from predictability, even though we don't like the results. We may fear change because it's unfamiliar and out of our control once the process starts.

But change is inevitable in a relationship. Even when we stay the same, the longevity of a pattern changes us and our partner. We have the right and the power to change our patterns in a direction that suits us. It takes only one small step by one person in a relationship to set the direction of change.

Personal Affirmations

I, (your name), have the courage to begin the changes I want.

You, (your name), have the courage to begin the changes you want.

(Your name) has the courage to begin the changes she/he wants.

We, (your name) and (other's name), have the courage to begin the changes we want.

Reciprocal Affirmations

I, (your name), have the courage to begin the changes I want.

You, (other's name), have the courage to begin the changes you want.

We, (your name) and (other's name), have the courage to begin the changes we want.

(Your name) and (other's name) have the courage to begin the changes they want.

If things go our way, it's easy to feel good. But you probably know people whose spirits aren't lifted by good events. And you may know people who remain cheerful through adversity. It's from within that we get good feelings. We can choose to respond to our world and our relationships with positive feelings.

For example, if someone's behavior bothers us we might feel angry and disappointed. But we may also feel hopeful. If we use this good feeling to help us communicate effectively with the other, then we might also feel grateful for their listening. Good feelings are a conscious choice and build one on another.

Personal Affirmations
I, (your name), choose to have good feelings.
You, (your name), choose to have good feelings.
(Your name) chooses to have good feelings.
We, (your name) and (other's name), choose to have good feelings.

Reciprocal Affirmations
I, (your name), choose to have good feelings.
You, (other's name), choose to have good feelings.
We, (your name) and (other's name), choose to have good feelings.
(Your name) and (other's name) choose to have good feelings.

Sharing experiences enriches our relationships. Taking a walk, meeting new people, reading the same book, exploring a museum, buying a greeting card and finding a new restaurant are a few ways we can create common experience.

Shared experiences give us time together when we're both in an expansive state — growing, learning, enjoying. They show us each other in a different light. We see a new side in the other or find a new side in ourselves to share. We appreciate each other in new ways and find more to enjoy.

We need not look for or avoid differences. Experiences are enriched by a different point of view and the presence of a loved one.

Personal Affirmations
I, (your name), enjoy shared experiences with others.
You, (your name), enjoy shared experiences with others.
(Your name) enjoys shared experiences with others.
We, (your name) and (other's name), enjoy shared experiences with others.

Reciprocal Affirmations
I, (your name), enjoy shared experiences with you.
You, (other's name), enjoy shared experiences with me.
We, (your name) and (other's name), enjoy shared experiences with each other.
(Your name) and (other's name) enjoy shared experiences with each other.

Sometimes we think we should like someone or do something because the other in a relationship likes them or wants to do it. While it's true that sharing interests or activities can help a relationship, it only helps if it's not forced or done with a sense of duty.

It's okay for me to have separate interests. It's all right for me to have my own friendships with other people. I can share or not share these interests and friendships with another as I choose.

Personal Affirmations

I, (your name), can have independent friendships and activities.

You, (your name), can have independent friendships and activities.

(Your name) can have independent friendships and activities.

We, (your name) and (other's name), can each have independent friendships and activities.

Reciprocal Affirmations

I, (your name), can have independent friendships and activities.

You, (other's name), can have independent friendships and activities.

We, (your name) and (other's name), can each have independent friendships and activities.

(Your name) and (other's name) can each have independent friendships and activities.

Each person chooses their own path in life regarding their health. We may feel we know what is best for another and offer them advice on their health. It's natural to want those we care about to live long and healthy lives.

But if someone close doesn't take our advice, it does no good to nag. The other is unlikely to yield to increasing pressure from us. Instead our relationship will suffer and we will have less influence, not more. The relationship motivates our insistent advice, yet we can't enjoy the relationship if we're constantly nagging. Once we share any useful information, it's up to the other to take it or leave it.

Personal Affirmations

I, (your name), free others to take or leave my advice.

You, (your name), free others to take or leave your advice.

(Your name) frees others to take or leave her/his advice.

We, (your name) and (other's name), free others to take or leave our advice.

Reciprocal Affirmations

I, (your name), free you to take or leave my advice.

You, (other's name), free me to take or leave your advice.

We, (your name) and (other's name), free each other to take or leave the other's advice.

(Your name) and (other's name) free each other to take or leave the other's advice.

Sometimes I get angry at another. I want to yell and scream and express my feelings. I want the other to know how stupid they've been and that it wouldn't have happened if they had listened to me. I feel helpless or frustrated that they didn't take my advice, didn't do things the way I would have, or didn't do it the way they should have — the right way.

I need to forgive the other person for their mistake or for making a choice different from what I might have made. I need to forgive myself for thinking I am responsible for or should control the other person's actions.

Personal Affirmations

I, (your name), examine my anger and let go of it.
You, (your name), examine your anger and let go of it.
(Your name) examines her/his anger and lets go of it.
We, (your name) and (other's name), examine our anger and let go of it.

Reciprocal Affirmations

I, (your name), examine my anger and let go of it.
You, (other's name), examine your anger and let go of it.
We, (your name) and (other's name), examine our anger and let go of it.
(Your name) and (other's name) examine their anger and let go of it.

In our sexual relationships we share our adventures together. If there is stress in our sexual interaction, attempts to manipulate our feelings with fantasy, surprise, variety and so forth will not be as helpful in the long run as getting back to basics.

The basics of good sex include feeling good about ourselves and the other. The better we know and like ourselves and the other, the more secure, comfortable, playful and adventurous we will feel.

Trying hard for good sex will yield less success than backing up a little and exploring each other and the world through words, touch and shared experiences.

Personal Affirmations

I, (your name), explore my lover at my own pace.

You, (your name), explore your lover at your own pace.

(Your name) explores her/his lover at her/his own pace.

We, (your name) and (other's name), explore each other at our own pace.

Reciprocal Affirmations

I, (your name), explore you at my own pace.

You, (other's name), explore me at your own pace.

We, (your name) and (other's name), explore each other at our own pace.

(Your name) and (other's name) explore each other at their own pace.

Society's stratification in school, workplace and neighborhood exposes us mainly to people of roughly the same age and circumstances. Yet there is much to learn from those of different ages and circumstances. We can tap those perspectives by encouraging such relationships.

For instance, children and teenagers — whether our own, relatives or neighbors — often have a fresh outlook, aren't cynical and can see right through phoniness. Cultivating friendships with young people gives us an opportunity to grow in these areas.

Personal Affirmations

I, (your name), cultivate friendships with younger people.

You, (your name), cultivate friendships with younger people.

(Your name) cultivates friendships with younger people.

We, (your name) and (other's name), cultivate friendships with younger people.

Reciprocal Affirmations

I, (your name), cultivate friendships with younger people.

You, (other's name), cultivate friendships with younger people.

We, (your name) and (other's name), cultivate friendships with younger people.

(Your name) and (other's name) cultivate friendships with younger people.

Sometimes we forget the significance of a simple hug. In our modern technological age, we interact with many strangers and we focus on causes and effects that can be explained. Hugs have fallen by the wayside. Yet a friendly or tender embrace offered by an acquaintance or loved one can be extremely beneficial to our state of mind.

We can ask for hugs and we can give them. Who in our lives would we like to have give us a hug? Our spouse, child, friend? Would we feel comfortable asking them? Or giving them one ourselves? If we're unaccustomed to hugs, we may want to rehearse: "Can I give you a hug?" or "Would you give me a hug?"

Personal Affirmations

I, (your name), give and get hugs easily.

You, (your name), give and get hugs easily.

(Your name) gives and gets hugs easily.

We, (your name) and (other's name), give and get hugs easily.

Reciprocal Affirmations

I, (your name), hug you easily.

You, (other's name), hug me easily.

We, (your name) and (other's name), hug each other easily.

(Your name) and (other's name) hug each other easily.

We are often faced with trying to comfort a friend, lover or child who is distressed, frustrated, depressed, angry or sad. Many of us have been raised to respond with sympathy: "You poor dear." But that response doesn't help the other feel good about themselves. It keeps them feeling down.

Empathy, not sympathy, gives the support and comfort we would like to give. "That's really frustrating to you." "That's really upsetting to you." These responses acknowledge the other's feelings, validate them and allow the other to feel good about them. That dose of self-esteem at a difficult time truly provides comfort and support.

Personal Affirmations
I, (your name), respond with empathy.
You, (your name), respond with empathy.
(Your name) responds with empathy.
We, (your name) and (other's name), respond with empathy.

Reciprocal Affirmations
I, (your name), respond to you with empathy.
You, (other's name), respond to me with empathy.
We, (your name) and (other's name), respond to each other with empathy.
(Your name) and (other's name) respond to each other with empathy.

Do our relationships bring us joy and pleasure? If not, why not? We're entitled to enjoy all of our life. We can change the parts we don't enjoy, including our relationships.

Changing a relationship starts with changing our end of it. Once our end is changed, even if the other person doesn't change, the relationship will be changed. And its effect on us will be changed. We can make changes so we enjoy all of our life and all of our relationships.

Personal Affirmations

I, (your name), initiate change in any relationship I don't enjoy.

You, (your name), initiate change in any relationship you don't enjoy.

(Your name) initiates change in any relationship she/he doesn't enjoy.

We, (your name) and (other's name), initiate change in any relationship we don't enjoy.

Reciprocal Affirmations

I, (your name), initiate change in any aspect of our relationship I don't enjoy.

You, (other's name), initiate change in any aspect of our relationship you don't enjoy.

We, (your name) and (other's name), initiate change in any aspect of our relationship we don't enjoy.

(Your name) and (other's name) initiate change in any aspect of their relationship they don't enjoy.

Often the people close to us ask the wrong questions. They ask us what we think, what we would do, what they should do or what's right. The closer we feel to them, the more eager we are to have them do the best thing. In our eagerness, we get in their way.

We each can solve our own problems and only our own problems. When someone asks our advice, our best response is empathy. We need to show our respect for their feelings, our faith in their resourcefulness and our willingness to share any information we have, but avoid telling them what to do. When we give empathy instead of solutions, others discover their own solutions and are happier for it.

Personal Affirmations

I, (your name), let others solve their own problems.

You, (your name), let others solve their own problems.

(Your name) lets others solve their own problems.

We, (your name) and (other's name), let others solve their own problems.

Reciprocal Affirmations

I, (your name), let you solve your own problems.

You, (other's name), let me solve my own problems.

We, (your name) and (other's name), let each other solve our own problems.

(Your name) and (other's name) let each other solve their own problems.

If we're highly critical of our bodies, we may be sabotaging ourselves in our physical relationships. If we're waiting until we're perfect before we feel attractive to the opposite sex, we tend to project insecurity, which makes us less attractive.

We can feel more attractive and as a result become so by accepting our bodies as they are. At any given moment, even if we aren't at our ideal weight, state of fitness or health, we can be attractive by projecting our energy and love from within. Our bodies are never static but always changing. They will reflect a positive self-image more quickly than obey our impatient self-criticism.

Personal Affirmations

I, (your name), appreciate rather than criticize my body.

You, (your name), appreciate rather than criticize your body.

(Your name) appreciates rather than criticizes her/his body.

We, (your name) and (other's name), appreciate rather than criticize our bodies.

Reciprocal Affirmations

I, (your name), appreciate rather than criticize my body.

You, (other's name), appreciate rather than criticize your body.

We, (your name) and (other's name), appreciate rather than criticize our bodies.

(Your name) and (other's name) appreciate rather than criticize their bodies.

If you're giving kindness, caring and trust, you have every right to expect it back from your important relationships. It's unhealthy to feel that you're constantly giving to others. You need to give to someone who can and will reciprocate.

We need to find some people who reciprocate for us, even if it means changing or ending at least some of our taking relationships. We have every right to have our needs fulfilled while we help fulfill the needs of others. We need to consider whether our relationships are positive for us.

Personal Affirmations

I, (your name), look for people who reciprocate kindness.

You, (your name), look for people who reciprocate kindness.

(Your name) looks for people who reciprocate kindness.

We, (your name) and (other's name), look for people who reciprocate kindness.

Reciprocal Affirmations

I, (your name), look for people who reciprocate kindness.

You, (other's name), look for people who reciprocate kindness.

We, (your name) and (other's name), look for people who reciprocate kindness.

(Your name) and (other's name) look for people who reciprocate kindness.

It can be just as hard to share positive feelings as negative ones. We may assume anger, guilt or other negative feelings reveal deep dark secrets or elicit negative responses, while positive feelings are more acceptable and less provocative. Assuming positive feelings are easier to share, we tend to spend less effort on venting them.

But sharing positive feelings is a communications skill that can be developed like any other. We can become more effective at getting the satisfaction we seek when we tell someone we feel happy. The first step is to accept that we must tell the other. We shouldn't expect the other to read our mind and meet our mood.

Personal Affirmations
I, (your name), like to share my positive feelings.
You, (your name), like to share your positive feelings.
(Your name) likes to share her/his positive feelings.
We, (your name) and (other's name), like to share our positive feelings.

Reciprocal Affirmations
I, (your name), like to share my positive feelings with you.
You, (other's name), like to share your positive feelings with me.
We, (your name) and (other's name), like to share our positive feelings with each other.
(Your name) and (other's name) like to share their positive feelings with each other.

Some people always see the bright side of things while others can invariably find something to complain about. Often we take the complaints of those close to us too seriously. We change our plans and redirect our effort to solve the problem the other complained of, only to find them complaining about something else. They may even complain that we change our plans too much!

If someone close sees a problem where we see none, it's not our responsibility to solve it. And the more regularly we choose to find the bright side, the more likely the other is to discover that they too can choose not to find complaints.

Personal Affirmations

I, (your name), don't let others' complaints distract me.

You, (your name), don't let others' complaints distract you.

(Your name) doesn't let others' complaints distract her/him.

We, (your name) and (other's name), don't let others' complaints distract us.

Reciprocal Affirmations

I, (your name), don't let your complaints distract me.

You, (other's name), don't let my complaints distract you.

We, (your name) and (other's name), don't let each other's complaints distract us.

(Your name) and (other's name) don't let each other's complaints distract them.

When we have superior knowlege or experience, we often want to give advice to those we love. Especially when they ask for it, we are quick to speak of "should," "ought to," "must" or "have to." But everyone is capable of finding their own solutions. Our advice can interfere. If someone acts on our advice, even if it's good advice, the temporary success will not make up for the injury to the person's confidence in finding future solutions.

We show our love by giving advice as options and suggestions, not orders; by sharing the information and experience we have; and by affirming the other's inner knowledge of what is best and their power to decide for themselves.

Personal Affirmations

I, (your name), give advice in a validating way.
You, (your name), give advice in a validating way.
(Your name) gives advice in a validating way.
We, (your name) and (other's name), give advice in a validating way.

Reciprocal Affirmations

I, (your name), give you advice in a validating way.
You, (other's name), give me advice in a validating way.
We, (your name) and (other's name), give each other advice in a validating way.
(Your name) and (other's name) give each other advice in a validating way.

Communicating in a way that is positive and supportive to both parties is natural for some lucky people, but more difficult for others. Learning some of the tools of good communication can help us.

Eye contact is one of the most effective communication tools available. Eye contact is looking the other straight in the eye rather than averting our gaze or exploring the room with our eyes. It gives the other a sense that we are focused on them, paying attention, concentrating on them and the topic — that we care.

Personal Affirmations

I, (your name), look into the eyes of those I talk to.

You, (your name), look into the eyes of those you talk to.

(Your name) looks into the eyes of those she/he talks to.

We, (your name) and (other's name), look into the eyes of those we talk to.

Reciprocal Affirmations

I, (your name), look into your eyes when I talk to you.

You, (other's name), look into my eyes when you talk to me.

We, (your name) and (other's name), look into each other's eyes when we talk.

(Your name) and (other's name) look into each other's eyes when they talk.

We often have trouble expressing our negative feelings in a healthy way. We try to learn, through this book and otherwise, how to do it. But do we ever feel alone when things are good? Do others attack us when we try to tell them our good news? Many of us need to learn how to express positive feelings in a healthy way that won't turn others off.

The same communication skills we use for expressing our negative feelings can be used to express our positive feelings.

Personal Affirmations

I, (your name), use my communication skills to express my good feelings.

You, (your name), use your communication skills to express your good feelings.

(Your name) uses her/his communication skills to express her/his good feelings.

We, (your name) and (other's name), use our communication skills to express our good feelings.

Reciprocal Affirmations

I, (your name), use my communication skills to express my good feelings to you.

You, (other's name), use your communication skills to express your good feelings to me.

We, (your name) and (other's name), use our communication skills to express our good feelings to each other.

(Your name) and (other's name) use their communication skills to express their good feelings to each other.

We each have special gifts that make us unique. We may have hunches about what they are, but we may be waiting for others to recognize them before we really do anything with them. Or we may try to be the perfect mate or friend and ignore our special gifts, only to feel unappreciated.

It's our job to know our special gifts, to develop them and to offer them to others without false humility. While balance is important, being well-rounded does not mean ignoring our uniqueness. Whether it's organizing, brainstorming, listening, entertaining or whatever, let others know your inclinations. Offer your gifts to others for your own sake and you will find greater appreciation.

Personal Affirmations

I, (your name), offer my gifts for my own sake.

You, (your name), offer your gifts for your own sake.

(Your name) offers her/his gifts for her/his own sake.

We, (your name) and (other's name), each offer our gifts for our own sakes.

Reciprocal Affirmations

I, (your name), offer you my gifts for my own sake.

You, (other's name), offer me your gifts for your own sake.

We, (your name) and (other's name), offer our gifts to each other for our own sakes.

(Your name) and (other's name) offer their gifts to each other for their own sakes.

Surveys show that people believe a sense of humor is a major factor in attracting them to another. And we all appreciate friends as well as lovers with a sense of humor. Why is a sense of humor so important?

A sense of humor allows us to laugh at ourselves and our situation. It prevents us from taking everything so seriously. It helps us put things in perspective. When we're able to do that, we enjoy life more and are more fun to be with. That means better relationships.

Personal Affirmations

I, (your name), have a good sense of humor.

You, (your name), have a good sense of humor.

(Your name) has a good sense of humor.

We, (your name) and (other's name), have good senses of humor.

Reciprocal Affirmations

I, (your name), have a good sense of humor.

You, (other's name), have a good sense of humor.

We, (your name) and (other's name), each have good senses of humor.

(Your name) and (other's name) each have good senses of humor.

In our relationships we find it difficult to change our habits of thought and action. It's hard to be less critical, less argumentative, less self-pitying and less demanding. Change becomes easier when we try to crowd out the behaviors we don't want with new ones. I can destroy the power of old negative thinking by giving time to meditation, affirmations, inspirational reading, attentive listening and sharing of feelings.

I can crowd out negative actions each day by doing one generous thing, one helpful thing, one act of listening to another, one expression of empathy or one action toward a long-held goal. At the end of the day, I find I've changed with no struggle, but with ease and grace.

Personal Affirmations

I, (your name), fill my life with positive thoughts and actions.

You, (your name), fill your life with positive thoughts and actions.

(Your name) fills her/his life with positive thoughts and actions.

We, (your name) and (other's name), each fill our lives with positive thoughts and actions.

Reciprocal Affirmations

I, (your name), fill my life with positive thoughts and actions.

You, (other's name), fill your life with positive thoughts and actions.

We, (your name) and (other's name), each fill our lives with positive thoughts and actions.

(Your name) and (other's name) fill their lives with positive thoughts and actions.

Many of us act differently to different people depending on our relationship. If we meet someone we perceive as important, such as a high government official or the owner of the company we work for, we're deferential. We hold back and don't say certain things we might normally say. If we meet someone we consider our equal, we're more comfortable and may act normally. If we meet someone we perceive as below us in economic or social status, are we as comfortable and do we act normally?

Our perception of ourselves and the other affects our relationship. If we change our perception, we can change the relationship. We can look at everyone's good side.

Personal Affirmations

I, (your name), see the good in others.

You, (your name), see the good in others.

(Your name) sees the good in others.

We, (your name) and (other's name), see the good in others.

Reciprocal Affirmations

I, (your name), see the good in you.

You, (other's name), see the good in me.

We, (your name) and (other's name), see the good in each other.

(Your name) and (other's name) see the good in each other.

When we offer our skills, knowledge or other gifts to others, we get our greatest satisfaction when they value us where we value ourselves. We may be highly skilled at cooking, for example. Perhaps it was a duty that fell to us early in our childhood home. Others may appreciate our good cooking and even shower us with appreciation. But if we value ourselves more for other skills, like good listening, gardening or inspiring children, we need to develop and offer these skills, even if at first we get less appreciation.

If we put our time and effort into manifesting those parts of ourselves we like most, others will like us better and we will like others better.

Personal Affirmations

I, (your name), am valued more and more where I value myself.

You, (your name), are valued more and more where you value yourself.

(Your name) is valued more and more where she/he values herself/himself.

We, (your name) and (other's name), are valued more and more where we value ourselves.

Reciprocal Affirmations

I, (your name), value you more and more where you value yourself.

You, (other's name), value me more and more where I value myself.

We, (your name) and (other's name), value each other where we value ourselves.

(Your name) and (other's name) value each other where they value themselves.

No matter how hard we want to work at improving our relationships, we can benefit from learning to be playful in them also. We need to be unafraid of being playful, spontaneous, surprising and light-hearted. If we or our partner are uneasy with these moods, it may be because they imply there is no one right way to do things. We have options and alternatives at every moment.

Children know that play is the essence of freedom. In play we explore options without judgment or serious commitment. We release ourselves from straight-line thinking and stretch our possibilities.

Personal Affirmations
I, (your name), am playful in my relationships.
You, (your name), are playful in your relationships.
(Your name) is playful in her/his relationships.
We, (your name) and (other's name), are playful in our relationships.

Reciprocal Affirmations
I, (your name), am playful in our relationship.
You, (other's name), are playful in our relationship.
We, (your name) and (other's name), are playful in our relationship.
(Your name) and (other's name) are playful in their relationship.

What do we want most from a relationship? Surely we want support, a feeling of belonging, peace and companionship. We also want fun, pleasure and laughter. Each of us is entitled to have these things. Too often we think peace and support are all we can attain or all we may deserve.

But unmitigated joy is our birthright. Our relationships are the most satisfying place to develop and express that state of being. We begin by looking for the bright side of things and people and by letting go of any secret fear that, if we stop monitoring the dark side, it will take us over.

Personal Affirmations

I, (your name), am entitled to unmitigated joy.

You, (your name), are entitled to unmitigated joy.

(Your name) is entitled to unmitigated joy.

We, (your name) and (other's name), are entitled to unmitigated joy.

Reciprocal Affirmations

I, (your name), am entitled to unmitigated joy.

You, (other's name), are entitled to unmitigated joy.

We, (your name) and (other's name), are entitled to unmitigated joy.

(Your name) and (other's name) are entitled to unmitigated joy.

In a sexual relationship, we often expect the other to meet our needs, help us escape from our cares and build our self-esteem. But sex is a form of communication. It requires a sharing between equals — expressing and listening to each other's thoughts and feelings, but never taking responsibility for the other's choices.

If we ask the other to take responsibility for our sexual enjoyment, sex becomes burdensome and ultimately unsatisfying. Instead we must take full responsibility for the quality of our sexual experience. This builds self-esteem and steadily increases our capacity for sexual enjoyment.

Personal Affirmations

I, (your name), am responsible for my sexual enjoyment.

You, (your name), are responsible for your sexual enjoyment.

(Your name) is responsible for her/his sexual enjoyment.

We, (your name) and (other's name), are each responsible for our own sexual enjoyment.

Reciprocal Affirmations

I, (your name), am responsible for my own sexual enjoyment.

You, (other's name), are responsible for your own sexual enjoyment.

We, (your name) and (other's name), are each responsible for our own sexual enjoyment.

(Your name) and (other's name) are each responsible for their own sexual enjoyment.

In despair, we trap ourselves in a vicious cycle of isolation and low self-esteem. We feel neglected and unloved and avoid contact with others because we can't stand more rejection. Or we've had serious setbacks and disappointments and stop trying because we've lost faith in ourselves and in the universe to provide.

To break the vicious cycle we must find ways to increase our self-esteem and reduce our isolation. We can build self-esteem by affirming our humanity, our feelings, our foibles and our dreams. We can laugh at ourselves. We can count our blessings. And we can connect with others. We can reach out and share our feelings. That connection rebuilds our hope.

Personal Affirmations

I, (your name), find hope in my humanity and con-
    nectedness.

You, (your name), find hope in your humanity and
    connectedness.

(Your name) finds hope in her/his humanity and con-
    nectedness.

We, (your name) and (other's name), find hope in our
    humanity and connectedness.

Reciprocal Affirmations

I, (your name), find hope in my humanity and con-
    nectedness.

You, (other's name), find hope in your humanity and
    connectedness.

We, (your name) and (other's name), find hope in our
    humanity and connectedness.

(Your name) and (other's name) find hope in their
    humanity and connectedness.

We can get just as bottled up with good feelings as with bad. We may assume bad feelings need to be expressed to give us some relief, while we ought to be able to handle good feelings by ourselves. But vibrant health requires sharing just as disease requires relief. We're entitled to share our good cheer, little triumphs and moments of contentment. Too often, if these things find no outlet, we turn to false rewards and empty or destructive symbols of fun like overeating, drinking or shopping sprees.

We need to seek out people who can listen and appreciate our joy. Friends in good fortune are as important as friends in adversity.

Personal Affirmations

I, (your name), seek out people to share my joy.
You, (your name), seek out people to share your joy.
(Your name) seeks out people to share her/his joy.
We, (your name) and (other's name), seek out people to share our joy.

Reciprocal Affirmations

I, (your name), seek you out to share my joy.
You, (other's name), seek me out to share your joy.
We, (your name) and (other's name), seek out each other to share our joy.
(Your name) and (other's name) seek out each other to share their joy.

How do we express our good feelings to others? It seems obvious that we just tell them how we feel. Have we tried it, only to be met with a cold stare or with, "How come you're Mary Poppins today?" How do we express our good feelings so others will listen?

First, we try to identify our particular feeling, be it warm, joyous, appreciated, lusty, energized or something else. Then we take care not to relate it to the other's conduct such as, "I feel happy when you're not yelling at me," but instead to express it as it relates to our own feelings such as, "I feel great when I get along with you."

Personal Affirmations

I, (your name), share my good feelings with others.
You, (your name), share your good feelings with others.
(Your name) shares her/his good feelings with others.
We, (your name) and (other's name), share our good feelings with others.

Reciprocal Affirmations

I, (your name), share my good feelings with you.
You, (other's name), share your good feelings with me.
We, (your name) and (other's name), share our good feelings with each other.
(Your name) and (other's name) share their good feelings with each other.

Great sex takes two elements, the physical and the emotional, just as it takes two people. Great sex is more than great technique. There's a strong and important emotional element.

Feeling close to our sex partner is the emotional element. We need to feel close, not as a result of sex, but independent of and prior to sex. We feel close from mutual sharing, caring, concern and commitment. Feeling close enhances the physical element and makes good sex great.

Personal Affirmations

Feeling close to my partner helps me, (your name), have great sex.

Feeling close to your partner helps you, (your name), have great sex.

Feeling close to her/his partner helps (your name) have great sex.

Feeling close to each other helps us, (your name) and (other's name), have great sex.

Reciprocal Affirmations

Feeling close to you helps me, (your name), have great sex.

Feeling close to me helps you, (other's name), have great sex.

Feeling close to each other helps us, (your name) and (other's name), have great sex.

Feeling close to each other helps (your name) and (other's name) have great sex.

What is this state of "being"? In today's slang it's often confused with vegetating. Vegetating is turning off worldly cares and anesthetizing one's senses. It might be plopping in front of the TV after a hard day and watching just anything so you don't have to think about the day gone by or that tomorrow might be the same.

"Being" is living in the moment with heightened awareness. It's appreciating and being totally tuned in to what's happening. It's not worrying about the past or the future, but enjoying the here and now.

Personal Affirmations

I, (your name), enjoy the here and now.

You, (your name), enjoy the here and now.

(Your name) enjoys the here and now.

We, (your name) and (other's name), enjoy the here and now.

Reciprocal Affirmations

I, (your name), enjoy the here and now with you.

You, (other's name), enjoy the here and now with me.

We, (your name) and (other's name), enjoy the here and now with each other.

(Your name) and (other's name) enjoy the here and now with each other.

We needn't be hard on ourselves about how much time we need to foster our personal growth. Sometimes someone close is jealous of our time and takes offense when we shut them out. But as long as we are honest with ourselves and sense a growing peace and light within, we need to trust the process of healing. If we are too short with ourselves and cut off needed time for meditation or calm, we only encourage the self-doubts that created the need for growth in the first place.

Instead we must trust our intuition of our needs for self-care or particular kinds of help, even if no one else ever trusted us that way.

Personal Affirmations

I, (your name), trust my intuition about time I need for myself.

You, (your name), trust your intuition about time you need for yourself.

(Your name) trusts her/his intuition about time she/he needs for herself/himself.

We, (your name) and (other's name), trust our intuitions about time we need for ourselves.

Reciprocal Affirmations

I, (your name), trust your intuition about time you need for yourself.

You, (other's name), trust my intuition about time I need for myself.

We, (your name) and (other's name), trust each other's intuition about time we need for ourselves.

(Your name) and (other's name) trust their intuitions about time they need for themselves.

Have we ever given our partner a book we wanted to read? Or have we ever received an appliance that the giver wanted to use? Many of us do the same sort of thing in our sexual relationship. We try to stimulate our partner by doing for them the things we want done for us.

Maybe we love to have our ear kissed. So we kiss our partner's ear. And our partner does things for us that don't really turn us on. Frequently we don't see that this is indirect communication — we don't realize that if we reversed roles we would have fabulously stimulating sex. Asking directly for what we want works better in all contexts, including sex.

Personal Affirmations

I, (your name), ask my sex partner for what I want.

You, (your name), ask your sex partner for what you want.

(Your name) asks her/his sex partner for what she/he wants.

We, (your name) and (other's name), ask our sex partner for what we want.

Reciprocal Affirmations

I, (your name), ask you for what I want in sex.

You, (other's name), ask me for what you want in sex.

We, (your name) and (other's name), ask each other for what we want in sex.

(Your name) and (other's name) ask each other for what they want in sex.

There's no magic formula for "being." It occurs when we let go of achieving, accomplishing and doing. It comes when we allow ourselves to do something just for us, just for pleasure. It might be a long walk in the country, not for exercise or to learn kinds of trees, but to enjoy being alive.

"Being" with another means you both are letting go at the same time. Relating with no demands and without an outside focus or reason is a new experience for many of us. Just "being" together adds a new dimension of pleasure to our relationship.

Personal Affirmations

I, (your name), am learning to let go and just be.

You, (your name), are learning to let go and just be.

(Your name) is learning to let go and just be.

We, (your name) and (other's name), are learning to let go and just be.

Reciprocal Affirmations

I, (your name), am learning to let go and just be with you.

You, (other's name), are learning to let go and just be with me.

We, (your name) and (other's name), are learning to let go and just be with each other.

(Your name) and (other's name) are learning to let go and just be with each other.

Dogs are well known for giving unconditional love to their owners. No matter what we do, our dog will love us. Our dog is always there, always glad to see us and always wants to spend time with us.

Though lacking in sophistication, a dog's love can teach us something about ways to encourage the giving and receiving unconditional love. We can learn a lot by observing our animal friends and putting their lessons of love to work in our own lives. Simplicity and genuineness are key.

Personal Affirmations

I, (your name), love simply and genuinely.

You, (your name), love simply and genuinely.

(Your name) loves simply and genuinely.

We, (your name) and (other's name), love simply and genuinely.

Reciprocal Affirmations

I, (your name), love you simply and genuinely.

You, (other's name), love me simply and genuinely.

We, (your name) and (other's name), love each other simply and genuinely.

(Your name) and (other's name) love each other simply and genuinely.

In our closest relationships we must be willing to share our deepest philosophy of life. We each have a way of looking at things, an image of cause and effect in our universe that we use to explain the workings of our lives. The more aware we are of this philosophy, the easier it is to help others get to know us and to discover our deepest connections.

Intimacy grows when we share our deepest longings, beliefs, convictions and triumphs. If we find our philosophies dramatically different, we need to make intelligent choices about how to proceed. If we are from very different walks of life, we can still have a deep, lasting relationship if we share a common philosophy.

Personal Affirmations

I, (your name), share my deepest philosophy with my partner.

You, (your name), share your deepest philosophy with your partner.

(Your name) shares her/his deepest philosophy with her/his partner.

We, (your name) and (other's name), share our deepest philosophies.

Reciprocal Affirmations

I, (your name), share my deepest philosophy with you.

You, (other's name), share your deepest philosophy with me.

We, (your name) and (other's name), share our deepest philosophies with each other.

(Your name) and (other's name) share their deepest philosophies with each other.

In our closest relationships we often act less courteously than we do with strangers. We may expect more of those closest and think we can do less. Or we may be tired from a long day of courtesy to others. Or we may believe courtesy is a public front to be dispensed with at home.

But courtesy builds the self-respect and respect for others essential to close relationships. I will be patient, gracious and grateful with those close to me. I will be clear about my feelings and requests. I will listen, give the other a turn to speak and avoid interrupting. I will respect physical space, possessions and choices. I will take time to say hello and goodbye.

Personal Affirmations

I, (your name), am most courteous to those closest to me.

You, (your name), are most courteous to those closest to you.

(Your name) is most courteous to those closest to her/him.

We, (your name) and (other's name), are most courteous to those closest to us.

Reciprocal Affirmations

I, (your name), am most courteous to you.

You, (other's name), are most courteous to me.

We, (your name) and (other's name), are most courteous to each other.

(Your name) and (other's name) are most courteous to each other.

Some days our problems seem so overwhelming we feel desperate. Maybe we feel trapped in an abusive relationship or in an extreme financial bind. We don't know what we can do but we feel we have to do something.

We need to express our feelings. Once we've shared our feelings and received some empathy, it won't seem like the end of the world anymore. By then we may see the humor in our extreme feelings. If we do see the humor and can laugh, we will feel better. Our problem will not have changed, but we won't be paralyzed with desperation. We'll be in a better position to deal with it.

Personal Affirmations

I, (your name), express any feelings of desperation.
You, (your name), express any feelings of desperation.
(Your name) expresses any feelings of desperation.
We, (your name) and (other's name), express any feelings of desperation.

Reciprocal Affirmations

I, (your name), express any feelings of desperation to you.
You, (other's name), express any feelings of desperation to me.
We, (your name) and (other's name), express any feelings of desperation to each other.
(Your name) and (other's name) express any feelings of desperation to each other.

If we react in unpredictable or destructive ways in our relationships, we need to look within. Looking deep into ourselves can arouse so much fear and anxiety that we turn away. But we have nothing to fear. Our inner explorations move only as fast as we're prepared to handle them. We have our own innate good timing. This can be the first of many positive realizations about ourselves.

Next we find that in most situations we have acted from good motives and with the best information we had. We can appreciate that. Gradually we discover that our mistakes are forgivable. Instead of a deep dark core that's fearful to behold, we find a spiritual being founded in love.

Personal Affirmations
I, (your name), look within without fear.
You, (your name), look within without fear.
(Your name) looks within without fear.
We, (your name) and (other's name), look within without fear.

Reciprocal Affirmations
I, (your name), look within myself without fear.
You, (other's name), look within yourself without fear.
We, (your name) and (other's name), each look within ourselves without fear.
(Your name) and (other's name) look within themselves without fear.

Remember when our parents used to tell us, "Don't talk to strangers"? We were preschoolers or in the early grades, and the underlying message was important to our safety. But have we let that childhood rule affect our ability to meet people and establish relationships in adult life?

Many of us are uncomfortable walking into a room full of strangers. If we look at our connection with the other person — a shared profession at the convention, shared employer at the national sales meeting, shared hobby at the flower show or shared friend at the party — we can be more comfortable meeting new people and establishing new relationships.

Personal Affirmations

I, (your name), look for my connection with other people.

You, (your name), look for your connection with other people.

(Your name) looks for her/his connection with other people.

We, (your name) and (other's name), look for our connections with other people.

Reciprocal Affirmations

I, (your name), look for my connection with other people.

You, (other's name), look for your connection with other people.

We, (your name) and (other's name), look for our connections with other people.

(Your name) and (other's name) look for their connections with other people.

When our views on a subject differ from those of another, we may not want to discuss them for fear of having a disagreement. Politics, for instance, is off limits as a topic in many close relationships, just as religion is off limits in many casual relationships. We don't want to risk an argument and perhaps weaken or end the relationship.

If we have the courage to talk about all subjects with the other and respect their views even if very different from our own, we can grow closer. The sharing and respect help build the relationship. We need to remember to keep things in perspective — our relationship is more important than convincing the other we're right.

Personal Affirmations
I, (your name), encourage and respect others' views.
You, (your name), encourage and respect others' views.
(Your name) encourages and respects others' views.
*We, (your name) and (other's name), encourage and
    respect each other's views.*

Reciprocal Affirmations
I, (your name), encourage and respect your views.
You, (other's name), encourage and respect my views.
*We, (your name) and (other's name), encourage and
    respect each other's views.*
*(Your name) and (other's name) encourage and
    respect each other's views.*

When we fail in our communication, it's often without even knowing it. We think we gave information to another or got them to do something, only to find out later that the other had a different understanding. Or we received information or agreed to do something, only to find out later we had a different understanding from the other.

A technique to help avoid misunderstandings is to talk enough about the background to give our information or request a context. If we both talk about the context, we'll know we're both on the same wavelength because we're speaking about the same thing.

Personal Affirmations

I, (your name), set the context to avoid misunderstandings.

You, (your name), set the context to avoid misunderstandings.

(Your name) sets the context to avoid misunderstandings.

We, (your name) and (other's name), set the context to avoid misunderstandings.

Reciprocal Affirmations

I, (your name), set the context to avoid misunderstandings.

You, (other's name), set the context to avoid misunderstandings.

We, (your name) and (other's name), set the context to avoid misunderstandings.

(Your name) and (other's name) set the context to avoid misunderstandings.

In a long-term relationship we each change at different times. This requires adjustment in our patterns. It's surprising how much more tension we experience from friction in everyday interactions than from weighty differences of perspective or principle.

Patterns of our life that seem satisfactory may still need adjustment. For example, in our morning routine, do we eat or dress first, and should we change it? Or in our evening routine, should we share our day's happenings and intimacy before or after we get ready for bed? If we think of our routines as fixed and correct, change is hard. If we are flexible and open to new possibilities, we can release a great deal of tension.

Personal Affirmations

I, (your name), review my routines with an open mind.

You, (your name), review your routines with an open mind.

(Your name) reviews her/his routines with an open mind.

We, (your name) and (other's name), review our routines with open minds.

Reciprocal Affirmations

I, (your name), review our routines with an open mind.

You, (other's name), review our routines with an open mind.

We, (your name) and (other's name), review our routines with open minds.

(Your name) and (other's name) review their routines with open minds.

When we want to share good feelings with another, the way we do it can make a big difference in their response. The simplest way is to use "I" messages. "I feel content when snow has fallen overnight." "I feel appreciated when you thank me for dinner." "I feel proud when we reach a decision without tension."

If instead we say, "Isn't the snow wonderful?" we might get a grumpy response. Or if we say, "For once you thanked me," we might provoke anger. Or if we say, "Look, we did it without tension this time!" the other might challenge our facts.

It's best to describe causes in a nonthreatening, matter-of-fact way and focus on the "I" messages.

Personal Affirmations

I, (your name), use "I" messages when I feel good.

You, (your name), use "I" messages when you feel good.

(Your name) uses "I" messages when she/he feels good.

We, (your name) and (other's name), use "I" messages when we feel good.

Reciprocal Affirmations

I, (your name), use "I" messages when I feel good.

You, (other's name), use "I" messages when you feel good.

We, (your name) and (other's name), use "I" messages when we feel good.

(Your name) and (other's name) use "I" messages when they feel good.

Each of us has the right to be left alone. We have the right to silence and time to ourselves. We have the right to withdraw from an emotionally provocative situation without giving any explanations for doing so. And we have the right to take time to ourselves without others second-guessing our motives or reading negative messages into our actions. If we mean to sulk and brood, then we must accept that we may provoke a response with our "fightin' silence." But otherwise we may disregard others' possible misinterpretations.

Honesty with ourselves is essential. When we know our boundaries and protect them, we're immune to manipulation.

Personal Affirmations
I, (your name), protect my boundaries.
You, (your name), protect your boundaries.
(Your name) protects her/his boundaries.
We, (your name) and (other's name), protect our boundaries.

Reciprocal Affirmations
I, (your name), protect my boundaries and respect yours.
You, (other's name), protect your boundaries and respect mine.
We, (your name) and (other's name), protect our own boundaries and respect each other's.
(Your name) and (other's name) protect their own boundaries and respect each other's.

Anxiety, discussion and arguing about finances or how to spend limited resources are common disruptions to a harmonious relationship. Virtually everyone has to make financial choices, and doing so when it affects others is a process few of us were taught. As children, many of us were taught that discussion of finances was taboo.

Calm communication about priorities and each person's view is the starting point. Giving each other some space and discretion, even if we have different views, is the midpoint. The end point is coming to an accommodation that each is comfortable with.

Personal Affirmations

I, (your name), work calmly toward agreement on finances.

You, (your name), work calmly toward agreement on finances.

(Your name) works calmly toward agreement on finances.

We, (your name) and (other's name), work calmly toward agreement on finances.

Reciprocal Affirmations

I, (your name), work calmly with you toward agreement on our finances.

You, (other's name), work calmly with me toward agreement on our finances.

We, (your name) and (other's name), work calmly toward agreement on our finances.

(Your name) and (other's name) work calmly toward agreement on their finances.

At different times we may have different feelings about another, such as a classic love/hate relationship. But what about having contradictory feelings at the same time about one another? We may feel love, lust and anger all at once or tenderness, concern and hurt at the same time.

It's normal to have multiple feelings about others, even at the same time. That's what makes relationships so complicated, rich and interesting. We need to deal with all our feelings and identify the ones that are temporary, such as hurt or anger, and the ones that are long-term, such as love and tenderness. It's the long-term feelings that should guide our actions.

Personal Affirmations

I, (your name), am guided by my long-term feelings.

You, (your name), are guided by your long-term feelings.

(Your name) is guided by her/his long-term feelings.

We, (your name) and (other's name), are guided by our long-term feelings.

Reciprocal Affirmations

I, (your name), am guided by my long-term feelings toward you.

You, (other's name), are guided by your long-term feelings toward me.

We, (your name) and (other's name), are guided by our long-term feelings toward each other.

(Your name) and (other's name) are guided by their long-term feelings toward each other.

When we have an intense feeling toward someone or something, we may get stuck on that feeling. We may believe we must express it, find an outlet for it, act on it or else feel guilty about it and suppress it. But if we allow ourselves a little time and attention, we discover we have multiple feelings in any situation. As soon as we acknowledge one feeling, another becomes apparent. For example, a sexual attraction to someone doesn't mean we must do anything. We need only acknowledge the feeling and move on in any direction we choose.

If we accept how rich an emotional life we have, we find more options and more freedom to choose what's right for us.

Personal Affirmations
I, (your name), have a rich abundance of feelings.
You, (your name), have a rich abundance of feelings.
(Your name) has a rich abundance of feelings.
We, (your name) and (other's name), have a rich abundance of feelings.

Reciprocal Affirmations
I, (your name), have a rich abundance of feelings.
You, (other's name), have a rich abundance of feelings.
We, (your name) and (other's name), have a rich abundance of feelings.
(Your name) and (other's name) have a rich abundance of feelings.

Just as music can soothe the mind and increase the integration of emotions and intellect, so our voices can have a beneficial effect on ourselves and others.

When we use a raspy, whining, choppy tone, we tend to create tension and adversity in ourselves and others. We shouldn't be surprised if others respond to us in critical or defensive modes. When we use a smooth, musical, open tone, we tend to create peace and harmony in ourselves and others.

I will keep my voice healthy and clear and think about my tone, rhythm and harmony as well as my words.

Personal Affirmations

I, (your name), have a beautiful voice.
You, (your name), have a beautiful voice.
(Your name) has a beautiful voice.
We, (your name) and (other's name), have beautiful voices.

Reciprocal Affirmations

I, (your name), love hearing your beautiful voice.
You, (other's name), love hearing my beautiful voice.
We, (your name) and (other's name), love hearing each other's beautiful voices.
(Your name) and (other's name) love hearing each other's beautiful voices.

When we feel tension in our relationships, we often fall into the habit of trying to control outside circumstances. We long to have things stay the same. We think if major changes come in jobs, living arrangements or time together, we'll be pushed beyond our limit and "lose it" altogether.

But the very essence of life is change. The unique character of living things is their ability to adjust to outside change and maintain a dynamic equilibrium.

We must seek our peace and stability from within. Knowing who we are and what we want makes change an adventure rather than a threat.

Personal Affirmations

I, (your name), look within for my stability.

You, (your name), look within for your stability.

(Your name) looks within herself/himself for her/his stability.

We, (your name) and (other's name), each look within ourselves for our stability.

Reciprocal Affirmations

I, (your name), look within for my stability.

You, (other's name), look within for your stability.

We, (your name) and (other's name), look within our relationship for stability between us.

(Your name) and (other's name) look within their relationship for stability between them.

When we make changes in one area of our lives, it may cause changes in other areas. For instance, a new job with more hours or more responsibility or a new relationship can use up the time we used to spend shopping, relaxing, exercising or playing with the kids.

New situations that cause lifestyle changes for us can produce fear and anxiety. We need to enter the new situation with confidence that everything can be worked out to our satisfaction. We also realize that, if it can't, we can again change the situation to one we are comfortable with.

Personal Affirmations

I, (your name), face new situations with confidence.

You, (your name), face new situations with confidence.

(Your name) faces new situations with confidence.

We, (your name) and (other's name), face new situations with confidence.

Reciprocal Affirmations

I, (your name), face new situations with confidence.

You, (other's name), face new situations with confidence.

We, (your name) and (other's name), face new situations with confidence.

(Your name) and (other's name) face new situations with confidence.

We learn a lot about others from their body language. If they habitually walk erect, appear confident, are cheerful and smile, we get a different impression than if they walk slouched and appear vulnerable and scared all the time. And our interactions my be different.

Our body language gives messages to others. Our relationships are affected by the messages we give others and their responses to us. If we're conscious that our body language reflects how we feel and make it consistent with the message we want to convey, we will have more successful interactions.

Personal Affirmations

I, (your name), make my body language consistent with my thoughts.

You, (your name), make your body language consistent with your thoughts.

(Your name) makes her/his body language consistent with her/his thoughts.

We, (your name) and (other's name), make our body language consistent with our thoughts.

Reciprocal Affirmations

I, (your name), make my body language consistent with my thoughts.

You, (other's name), make your body language consistent with your thoughts.

We, (your name) and (other's name), make our body language consistent with our thoughts.

(Your name) and (other's name) make their body language consistent with their thoughts.

Music has a mystical power to elicit emotion. Its patterns and rhythms evoke powerful images in our minds, change our moods, inspire us, anger us and amuse us. Music also synchronizes the left and right hemispheres of the brain, integrating our being and making us feel whole.

No matter what our taste in music, it enriches our lives. No matter what kind of music those around us like, we need not give up our own for their sakes. Nor should we object to the music in their lives.

If we appreciate how music can help create a healthy environment for all, we will be more willing to search for music we can enjoy together.

Personal Affirmations

I, (your name), enjoy music in my life.
You, (your name), enjoy music in your life.
(Your name) enjoys music in her/his life.
We, (your name) and (other's name), enjoy music in our lives.

Reciprocal Affirmations

I, (your name), appreciate how you enjoy music.
You, (other's name), appreciate how I enjoy music.
We, (your name) and (other's name), enjoy music together.
(Your name) and (other's name) enjoy music together.

Time seems very valuable. But it's only as valuable as we make it. If we fill our time with confusion, frustration, worry or wishing things were otherwise, it loses its value.

To make our time valuable, we must fill it with things that give us personal satisfaction. We must spend our time on things that are valuable to us. This means that time spent to choose our priorities for the day, the week or the month is well spent. Time to meditate, play with children, enjoy a good book or chat with a friend is also time made valuable. Instead of judging our time by its productiveness, we can make it personally valuable.

Personal Affirmations

I, (your name), make my time valuable to me.
You, (your name), make your time valuable to you.
(Your name) makes her/his time valuable to her/him.
We, (your name) and (other's name), each make our time valuable to us.

Reciprocal Affirmations

I, (your name), make my time valuable to me.
You, (other's name), make your time valuable to you.
We, (your name) and (other's name), make our time together valuable to us.
(Your name) and (other's name) make their time together valuable to them.

When a person close to us complains that they are overwhelmed with things to do to the point of immobilization and don't know where to turn, do we (a) offer helpful suggestions to get them started again, (b) give a pep talk, (c) say "Anyone with that much to do could feel overwhelmed," or (d) say "That's your problem"?

What the other is really looking for is someone to understand their feelings. In a word, they're seeking empathy. Response (d) is uncaring. Both (a) and (b) are likely to make the other feel more inadequate because they aren't getting things done. Response (c) is empathetic. It validates the other's feelings and lets them feel good about moving forward.

Personal Affirmations

I, (your name), validate others with empathy.

You, (your name), validate others with empathy.

(Your name) validates others with empathy.

We, (your name) and (other's name), validate others with empathy.

Reciprocal Affirmations

I, (your name), validate you with empathy.

You, (other's name), validate me with empathy.

We, (your name) and (other's name), validate each other with empathy.

(Your name) and (other's name) validate each other with empathy.

When we have a difficult decision to make, we often focus all our attention on it and try to wrestle it to a resolution. It can be more helpful to let it go for a while and put our mind on other things. Rather than force ourselves to decide, we can trust our inner processes to sort out any anxieties or blockages that prevent us from being comfortable with our choices or able to see our best choice.

If we give ourselves time and trust, decisions that seemed impossible become possible. Our anxiety may add urgency. When we calm ourselves, we find that most decisions can wait longer than we think while we become comfortable making them.

Personal Affirmations

I, (your name), give myself time in making decisions.

You, (your name), give yourself time in making decisions.

(Your name) gives herself/himself time in making decisions.

We, (your name) and (other's name), give ourselves time in making decisions.

Reciprocal Affirmations

I, (your name), give you time in making decisions.

You, (other's name), give me time in making decisions.

We, (your name) and (other's name), give each other time in making decisions.

(Your name) and (other's name) give each other time in making decisions.

Sometimes we drag through day after day tired from too little sleep. In our busy lives, we may think we just don't have time for more. We may not realize we're tired, irritable or in a bad mood, straining our physical system and making accidents more likely.

When we value ourselves and our relationships, we need to attach a high priority to things that are good for us and our health. Adequate sleep has a positive effect on our moods, attitudes and interactions. We need to recognize that it's an important priority and get the sleep we know we should have.

Personal Affirmations

I, (your name), give priority to myself and my sleep.

You, (your name), give priority to yourself and your sleep.

(Your name) gives priority to herself/himself and her/his sleep.

We, (your name) and (other's name), give priority to ourselves and our sleep.

Reciprocal Affirmations

I, (your name), give priority to myself and my sleep.

You, (other's name), give priority to yourself and your sleep.

We, (your name) and (other's name), give priority to ourselves and our sleep.

(Your name) and (other's name) give priority to themselves and their sleep.

Often we have goals in many different areas of our lives and find it hard to prioritize them. We may want to improve a relationship with someone close, get a promotion at work and reorganize our bedroom all at the same time. It may be tempting to put them all off. Or we may make half an effort at the one that seems easiest but lose interest when another looks more important.

When this happens, we need to reaffirm that we have the time, energy and skills to accomplish all we desire. Choose any one priority and dedicate a specific length of time to it. Then celebrate whatever you accomplish before you move on to another project.

Personal Affirmations

I, (your name), have the time, energy and skills I need for my goals.

You, (your name), have the time, energy and skills you need for your goals.

(Your name) has the time, energy and skills she/he needs for her/his goals.

We, (your name) and (other's name), have the time, energy and skills we need for our goals.

Reciprocal Affirmations

I, (your name), have the time, energy and skills I need for my goals.

You, (other's name), have the time, energy and skills you need for your goals.

We, (your name) and (other's name), have the time, energy and skills we need for our goals.

(Your name) and (other's name) have the time, energy and skills they need for their goals.

We really feel good when someone appreciates us. "Thanks for waiting up for me." "You did a great job with that customer." "I really appreciate that you got the plumbing fixed so quickly." Any of these are music to our ears and a boost to our self-esteem.

Just as we feel good when others appreciate us, others feel good when we appreciate them. Expressing our appreciation helps others feel better about themselves. It's easier to have a healthy relationship with someone who knows they are appreciated.

Personal Affirmations

I, (your name), express my appreciation of others.
You, (your name), express your appreciation of others.
(Your name) expresses her/his appreciation of others.
We, (your name) and (other's name), express our appreciation of others.

Reciprocal Affirmations

I, (your name), express my appreciation of you.
You, (other's name), express your appreciation of me.
We, (your name) and (other's name), express our appreciation of each other.
(Your name) and (other's name) express their appreciation of each other.

When we're stressed out by work or family, it can spill over and cause tension in our relationship unless we take steps to avoid it. We need to focus on enjoying the other however we do that.

We might think of the most enjoyable thing about the other, be it cuddling, talking, sharing music, sex or laughing together. Then we can go about enjoying it. Enjoying the other will help relieve our stress and avoid tension in our relationship. I will take a few minutes today and enjoy my partner.

Personal Affirmations

I, (your name), focus on enjoying my partner.
You, (your name), focus on enjoying your partner.
(Your name) focuses on enjoying her/his partner.
We, (your name) and (other's name), focus on enjoying each other.

Reciprocal Affirmations

I, (your name), focus on enjoying you.
You, (other's name), focus on enjoying me.
We, (your name) and (other's name), focus on enjoying each other.
(Your name) and (other's name) focus on enjoying each other.

Today and every day I have the power to change any relationship I have for the better. I also have the power to reaffirm or discard any relationship.

None of my relations with any person is limited by past behavior. I can change all or any part of my behavior in any relationship.

I will build on those parts of my relationships I see as healthy or fun, and I will discard those parts I see as counterproductive, burdensome, unhealthy or not fun.

Personal Affirmations

I, (your name), have the power to change my relationships for the better.

You, (your name), have the power to change your relationships for the better.

(Your name) has the power to change her/his relationships for the better.

We, (your name) and (other's name), have the power to change our relationships for the better.

Reciprocal Affirmations

I, (your name), have the power to change our relationship for the better.

You, (other's name), have the power to change our relationship for the better.

We, (your name) and (other's name), have the power to change our relationship for the better.

(Your name) and (other's name) have the power to change their relationship for the better.

I am willing to think about my relationships and to set goals for them and for my behavior in them.

My goals are the things I want most from the relationship. I am realistic in choosing those things that are most important to me. Some of them may be emotional support, sharing, empathy, companionship, fun and personal growth.

My life isn't dependent on any relationship. I don't expect anyone to save me in any situation.

I will maintain my freedom and individuality. The goals I choose for the relationship allow me that freedom.

Personal Affirmations

I, (your name), set realistic goals for my relations with others.

You, (your name), set realistic goals for your relations with others.

(Your name) sets realistic goals for her/his relations with others.

We, (your name) and (other's name), set realistic goals for our relations with others.

Reciprocal Affirmations

I, (your name), set realistic goals for my relations with you.

You, (other's name), set realistic goals for your relations with me.

We, (your name) and (other's name), set realistic goals for our relations with each other.

(Your name) and (other's name) set realistic goals for their relations with each other.

We make plans to give direction to our lives, to help us follow priorities and to look forward to the future. Plans aren't promises we must keep to ourselves or others. Nor are they goals we must pursue at all costs.

When we are connected to another, their needs and wants affect our plans in ways we can't predict or control. And our relationship has its own effects, independent of each of us.

When plans change, we need not fear the worst, that we may be unreliable, undedicated or poor planners. Stick-to-it-iveness is only as good as the present appropriateness of our plans. Flexibility allows us to let go of some plans in favor of our larger plan.

Personal Affirmations

I, (your name), stay flexible when I make plans that involve others.

You, (your name), stay flexible when you make plans that involve others.

(Your name) stays flexible when she/he makes plans that involve others.

We, (your name) and (other's name), stay flexible when we make plans that involve others.

Reciprocal Affirmations

I, (your name), stay flexible when I make plans that involve you.

You, (other's name), stay flexible when you make plans that involve me.

We, (your name) and (other's name), stay flexible when we make plans that involve each other.

(Your name) and (other's name) stay flexible when they make plans that involve each other.

As we commemorate the independence of our country, we can take the opportunity to examine our independence in all things. In our relationships we want to establish, maintain or reaffirm our independence.

What does it mean to be independent in a relationship? It means I make my own decisions based on what I want, not what others expect or what I may think would please them — though of course I can take these into account. It means I put myself and my needs first, giving myself the strength and self-esteem to be a good companion to others. It means I value my relationships because I value myself.

Personal Affirmations

I, (your name), affirm my independence today.
You, (your name), affirm your independence today.
(Your name) affirms her/his independence today.
We, (your name) and (other's name), affirm our independence today.

Reciprocal Affirmations

I, (your name), affirm my independence today.
You, (other's name), affirm your independence today.
We, (your name) and (other's name), affirm each other's independence today.
(Your name) and (other's name) affirm their independence today.

Often we cling to relationships that are no longer comfortable out of an exaggerated sense of obligation. Or we fear we won't find a better one and believe some relationship is better than none.

Relationships that fade because of distance or changed circumstances deserve to be mourned like any loss. So do relationships that no longer feel good because either we or the other has changed. Mourning and moving on are healthier for us than feeling guilty that we no longer feel the same as we once did. When we accept the loss, we can feel secure that conscious awareness of our present needs will lead us to new relationships that offer us greater comfort.

Personal Affirmations

I, (your name), let go of relationships that are no longer comfortable.

You, (your name), let go of relationships that are no longer comfortable.

(Your name) lets go of relationships that are no longer comfortable.

We, (your name) and (other's name), let go of relationships that are no longer comfortable.

Reciprocal Affirmations

I, (your name), let go of relationships that are no longer comfortable.

You, (other's name), let go of relationships that are no longer comfortable.

We, (your name) and (other's name), let go of relationships that are no longer comfortable.

(Your name) and (other's name) let go of relationships that are no longer comfortable.

I have a strong desire to feel close to others, be they lovers, children, parents or friends. When I give my full attention to someone close to me, I feel close to them.

I can give my full attention by first establishing eye contact. This focuses my attention. Then I will really listen or share something of myself — my feelings — or engage in a fun activity with the other.

My reward for giving a moment of my full attention is a feeling of closeness.

Personal Affirmations
Today I, (your name), will give someone close to me a moment of my full attention.

Today you, (your name), will give someone close a moment of your full attention.

Today (your name) will give someone close a moment of her/his full attention.

Today we, (your name) and (other's name), will give someone close a moment of our full attention.

Reciprocal Affirmations
Today I, (your name), will give you a moment of my full attention.

Today you, (your name), will give me a moment of your full attention.

Today we, (your name) and (other's name), will give each other a moment of our full attention.

Today (your name) and (other's name) will give each other a moment of their full attention.

Often we make up our minds about things quickly or absolutely and leave no room for the ideas of others. Or we hold no hope that others' ideas can help us and we give them scant attention. When we listen to the ideas of others, we benefit by sharing, by being close to another for a moment. We also encourage the other to share their ideas with us. Even if we don't like one idea, we may benefit from the next. And it's seldom that another's well-meant idea will not shed some light on our own.

I will cultivate my ability to listen attentively, to withhold judgment and to encourage others' ideas.

Personal Affirmations

I, (your name), open my mind and give full attention to others' ideas.

You, (your name), open your mind and give full attention to others' ideas.

(Your name) opens her/his mind and gives full attention to others' ideas.

We, (your name) and (other's name), open our minds and give full attention to others' ideas.

Reciprocal Affirmations

I, (your name), open my mind and give full attention to your ideas.

You, (other's name), open your mind and give full attention to my ideas.

We, (your name) and (other's name), open our minds and give full attention to each other's ideas.

(Your name) and (other's name) open their minds and give full attention to each other's ideas.

Successful relationships require communication, mutual support and commitment. Sometimes we want to try out a relationship, experiment with it to see if it will work. If we start with the attitude of wanting to see if it works before we fully commit to it, we are starting with one ingredient for success — commitment — missing.

We all make mistakes, but an appropriate level of commitment from the beginning makes success more likely. Instead of experimenting with a new relationship, we can commit ourselves to making it work.

Personal Affirmations

I, (your name), am committed to making my relationships work.

You, (your name), are committed to making your relationships work.

(Your name) is committed to making her/his relationships work.

We, (your name) and (other's name), are committed to making our relationships work.

Reciprocal Affirmations

I, (your name), am committed to making our relationship work.

You, (other's name), are committed to making our relationship work.

We, (your name) and (other's name), are committed to making our relationship work.

(Your name) and (other's name) are committed to making their relationship work.

Sometimes a problem, worry or task seems very important and takes much of my attention. Even when I'm dealing with other things, it's in the background. I can be impatient, short, insensitive or appear uncaring because my attention is focused on my preoccupation rather than the person at hand.

When I'm preoccupied, it's very important to recognize my feelings so they don't get in the way and unintentionally hurt my relationships with others. I need to express my feelings about the other rather than my feelings of preoccupation.

Personal Affirmations

I, (your name), won't let my preoccupations hurt my relationships.

You, (your name), won't let your preoccupations hurt your relationships.

(Your name) won't let her/his preoccupations hurt her/his relationships.

We, (your name) and (other's name), won't let our preoccupations hurt our relationships.

Reciprocal Affirmations

I, (your name), won't let my preoccupations hurt our relationship.

You, (other's name), won't let your preoccupations hurt our relationship.

We, (your name) and (other's name), won't let our preoccupations hurt our relationship.

(Your name) and (other's name) won't let their preoccupations hurt their relationship.

We all have little upsets or tiffs with other people. These seem normal because they happen frequently to most of the people we know. Most of them, however, are over inconsequential things that we often don't even remember after the upset. Wouldn't it be great to catch the little hurts at the beginning and avoid escalating them?

If we and the other mutually commit to avoid escalating little hurts into full-scale upsets, to slough them off as unthinking or unmeant comments rather than give them importance the speaker never intended, we can defuse many situations and avoid most upsets.

Personal Affirmations

I, (your name), don't let minor things upset me.
You, (your name), don't let minor things upset you.
(Your name) doesn't let minor things upset her/him.
We, (your name) and (other's name), don't let minor
    things upset us.

Reciprocal Affirmations

I, (your name), don't let minor things upset me.
You, (other's name), don't let minor things upset you.
We, (your name) and (other's name), don't let minor
    things upset us.
(Your name) and (other's name) don't let minor things
    upset them.

Actions which will have a big impact on a relationship call for mutual or joint decision-making. Mutual decisions are often difficult issues in relationships. Egos frequently get in the way. Such decisions can become shouting matches or times when one person gives in to avoid a confrontation.

To make mutual decisions without upset or rancor, both must acknowledge that there is more than one "right" way to do anything. Then we need to be open to options and list some of them. We need to be careful to keep our egos in check. Then we can mutually decide on the course of action which will best serve each of us and our relationship.

Personal Affirmations

I, (your name), recognize there is more than one right way.

You, (your name), recognize there is more than one right way.

(Your name) recognizes there is more than one right way.

We, (your name) and (other's name), recognize there is more than one right way.

Reciprocal Affirmations

I, (your name), recognize your way is one of the right ways.

You, (other's name), recognize my way is one of the right ways.

We, (your name) and (other's name), each recognize the other's way is one of the right ways.

(Your name) and (other's name) each recognize there is more than one right way.

I cannot love another more than I love myself. No matter how strong our relationship or how much I love another, my relationship with myself is the most important one I have. The name for that relationship is self-esteem.

If I spend all my time on my other relationships, my self-esteem suffers. When I take time for myself, I build my self-esteem. A walk in the woods, reading for pleasure, exercising, listening to music because I want to, getting a massage or whatever I like to do for myself makes me feel good.

When I feel good about myself, I can contribute to my relationships in a positive, healthy way.

Personal Affirmations

I, (your name), take time for my relationship with myself.

You, (your name), take time for your relationship with yourself.

(Your name) takes time for her/his relationship with herself/himself.

We, (your name) and (other's name), each take time for our relationships with ourselves.

Reciprocal Affirmations

I, (your name), give you time for your relationship with yourself.

You, (other's name), give me time for my relationship with myself.

We, (your name) and (other's name), give each other time for our relationships with ourselves.

(Your name) and (other's name) each take time for their relationships with themselves.

When we have a stable relationship that is comfortable and familiar, we often resist making changes in our lives that may affect the relationship, even though we feel the change would be good for us. In finding the courage to change in ways I know will benefit me, I will keep in mind that relationships themselves are always changing. Even apparently staying the same becomes different in quality when enough time has elapsed.

It's not a matter of choice between choosing change or avoiding it. Rather, it's a choice between having a part in directing change or being its passive object.

Personal Affirmations

I, (your name), take part in directing the changes in my life.

You, (your name), take part in directing the changes in your life.

(Your name) takes part in directing the changes in her/his life.

We, (your name) and (other's name), take part in directing the changes in our lives.

Reciprocal Affirmations

I, (your name), take part in directing the changes in my life.

You, (other's name), take part in directing the changes in your life.

We, (your name) and (other's name), take part in directing the changes in our lives.

(Your name) and (other's name) take part in directing the changes in their lives.

Sometimes I'm so concerned about the needs or expectations of others that I forget about what I want.

I am an independent person with my own needs and desires. I am important and I deserve to focus on myself and my wants. I feel good when I do focus on my wants. When I appreciate my value and my independence, I can make healthy contributions to my relationships.

It's okay for me to ask myself, others or the Universal Power for what I want.

Personal Affirmations

I, (your name), feel good about asking for what I want.

You, (your name), feel good about asking for what you want.

(Your name) feels good about asking for what she/he wants.

We, (your name) and (other's name), feel good about asking for what we want.

Reciprocal Affirmations

I, (your name), feel good about asking you for what I want.

You, (other's name), feel good about asking me for what you want.

We, (your name) and (other's name), feel good about asking each other for what we want.

(Your name) and (other's name) feel good about asking for what they want.

To build a relationship we need to take the risk of expressing our current challenges. How we feel about these challenges and the little decisions we make to meet them is a direct expression of who we are.

If we hide our concerns and challenges, we feel unsatisfied in the relationship, often without knowing why. We may believe the other will not be interested, will be turned off or will think we are selfish.

But if we take the risk of expressing our concerns and challenges, true friends will either have the same concerns, offer their moral support to us in ours or open up with their own concerns — and the relationship will grow.

Personal Affirmations

I, (your name), am open about my current challenges.

You, (your name), are open about your current challenges.

(Your name) is open about her/his current challenges.

We, (your name) and (other's name), are open about our current challenges.

Reciprocal Affirmations

I, (your name), am open with you about my current challenges.

You, (other's name), are open with me about your current challenges.

We, (your name) and (other's name), are open with each other about our current challenges.

(Your name) and (other's name) are open with each other about their current challenges.

We all need to take time away from our usual responsibilities, time for renewal. Vacations or getaway weekends serve this end. They lift some weight from our shoulders. No matter how great our responsibilities seem, we deserve time off and need it to clear our perspective and refocus.

Taking time away with another can help renew a relationship or keep it fresh. It gives us an opportunity to see the relationship in a different light — from a new perspective.

Personal Affirmations

I, (your name), take time off to renew myself and my relationships.

You, (your name), take time off to renew yourself and your relationships.

(Your name) takes time off to renew herself/himself and her/his relationships.

We, (your name) and (other's name), take time off to renew ourselves and our relationships.

Reciprocal Affirmations

I, (your name), take time off to renew myself and our relationship.

You, (other's name), take time off to renew yourself and our relationship.

We, (your name) and (other's name), take time off to renew ourselves and our relationship.

(Your name) and (other's name) take time off to renew themselves and their relationship.

Often we are afraid to share our feelings with another for fear of hurting their feelings, being misunderstood or arousing their anger or resentment. But not sharing our feelings denies the other the chance to know us better and to take our feelings into account in their decisions. It also makes us less open in the relationship and gradually estranges us.

We can share our feelings without these risks if we ask the other to listen patiently without judgment to all our feelings in a certain situation. Then we can express our love for them, our fear, the particular feeling that concerns us and also the more positive feelings that will emerge once we have shared.

Personal Affirmations

I, (your name), share my abundance of feelings with others.

You, (your name), share your abundance of feelings with others.

(Your name) shares her/his abundance of feelings with others.

We, (your name) and (other's name), share our abundance of feelings with others.

Reciprocal Affirmations

I, (your name), share my abundance of feelings with you.

You, (other's name), share your abundance of feelings with me.

We, (your name) and (other's name), share our abundance of feelings with each other.

(Your name) and (other's name) share their abundance of feelings with each other.

Each new day we awake to the beginning of the rest of our life. Each new day is a new opportunity to change those things we wish to change and affirm those things we want to maintain.

Each day is a new opportunity to work on our relationships. We can start new relationships and change, affirm or end old ones. We can express our love more freely and joyously to those we care about. We can enjoy all our relationships more.

Personal Affirmations

I, (your name), use my daily opportunity to improve my relationships.

You, (your name), use your daily opportunity to improve your relationships.

(Your name) uses her/his daily opportunity to improve her/his relationships.

We, (your name) and (other's name), use our daily opportunity to improve our relationships.

Reciprocal Affirmations

I, (your name), use my daily opportunity to improve our relationship.

You, (other's name), use your daily opportunity to improve our relationship.

We, (your name) and (other's name), use our daily opportunity to improve our relationship.

(Your name) and (other's name) use their daily opportunity to improve their relationship.

If my relationship demands too much energy, I will look at what it needs from me and what I do unnecessarily. If I try to please another, be like them or make them like me, I am trying to do the impossible. My commitment to our relationship is enough.

If I try to control another, make them better or fix up their life, I neglect myself. One life — mine — is all I can live. Mutual support is what I need to offer the other. If I insist on sharing the same tastes, choices and priorities, I'll love only a reflection of myself. Good communication is what I need to enjoy another.

Personal Affirmations

I, (your name), focus my energy on commitment, communication and mutual support.

You, (your name), focus your energy on commitment, communication and mutual support.

(Your name) focuses her/his energy on commitment, communication and mutual support.

We, (your name) and (other's name), each focus our energy on commitment, communication and mutual support.

Reciprocal Affirmations

I, (your name), focus my energy on commitment, communication and mutual support.

You, (other's name), focus your energy on commitment, communication and mutual support.

We, (your name) and (other's name), each focus our energy on commitment, communication and mutual support.

(Your name) and (other's name) each focus their energy on commitment, communication and mutual support.

Each of us has a natural sexuality that develops and matures along with other aspects of our being. It has unlimited potential for satisfaction if we are patient and let it unfold gradually, in harmony with our deepening love relationship. We may suppose that since sex is a physical act, its performance and results are finite. But we find our sexuality comes to full expression only in a deep, caring, mutually respectful and enjoyable relationship which takes time to establish. Even then it continues to change and increase our enjoyment with time.

Let's focus less on sexual technique and more on an increasingly satisfying relationship with our sex partner. This will make for better sex.

Personal Affirmations

I, (your name), enrich my sex life by enriching my love relationship.

You, (your name), enrich your sex life by enriching your love relationship.

(Your name) enriches her/his sex life by enriching her/his love relationship.

We, (your name) and (other's name), enrich our sex life by enriching our love relationship.

Reciprocal Affirmations

I, (your name), enrich my sex life by enriching our love relationship.

You, (other's name), enrich your sex life by enriching our love relationship.

We, (your name) and (other's name), enrich our sex life by enriching our love relationship.

(Your name) and (other's name) enrich their sex life by enriching their love relationship.

Our relationships often frustrate us because they are never complete or accomplished. Like a tree, they are always growing unless they are dying. Yet many of us come to think of sex or a sexual relationship as a goal. When we do this, we may be trying unproductively to attain it or become complacent or disappointed when we do.

A sexual relationship is just one way station on the path of physical intimacy, from the first glance and the first approach into each other's space to the ongoing sharing and wonderment of decades of sexual intimacy. Instead of goals, I will focus on the process of expressing my relationships through physical contact.

Personal Affirmations

I, (your name), cultivate healthy physical intimacy.

You, (your name), cultivate healthy physical intimacy.

(Your name) cultivates healthy physical intimacy.

We, (your name) and (other's name), cultivate healthy physical intimacy with each other.

Reciprocal Affirmations

I, (your name), cultivate healthy physical intimacy with you.

You, (other's name), cultivate healthy physical intimacy with me.

We, (your name) and (other's name), cultivate healthy physical intimacy with each other.

(Your name) and (other's name) cultivate healthy physical intimacy with each other.

When there is a difference in experience or knowledge in a relationship, we can ask ourselves who is the mentor and who the student? When one person is always seen as the mentor or the student, the relationship is strained.

In a healthy relationship, both people are sometimes mentor, sometimes student. I may be mentor on fashion design and sexual positions, student on touching and holiday celebrations. Even so, my mentor/student roles can change. Even as a student I have free choice as to whether to follow the mentor's advice.

A balance in mentor/student roles promotes balance in the relationship as well as mutual respect and excitement.

Personal Affirmations

I, (your name), am sometimes mentor and sometimes student, as I choose.

You, (your name), are sometimes mentor and sometimes student, as you choose.

(Your name) is sometimes mentor and sometimes student, as she/he chooses.

We, (your name) and (other's name), are sometimes mentor and sometimes student, as we choose.

Reciprocal Affirmations

I, (your name), am sometimes your mentor and sometimes your student.

You, (other's name), are sometimes my mentor and sometimes my student.

We, (your name) and (other's name), are sometimes mentor and sometimes student, as we choose.

(Your name) and (other's name) are sometimes mentor and sometimes student, as they choose.

Dealing with the multiple feelings we may have about another can be difficult. Sorting out which are temporary emotions, such as hurt and anger, and which are long-term emotions, such as love and caring, can be confusing.

Sharing our conflicting feelings by talking to another can be helpful. It gives us someone to listen, to hear us as we express our feelings. It also allows the other to get a deeper understanding of us. And if the other listens with empathy, it can help us understand our multiple feelings so we will act on the more important long-term feelings rather than the temporary ones.

Personal Affirmations

I, (your name), share my multiple feelings with another.

You, (your name), share your multiple feelings with another.

(Your name) shares her/his multiple feelings with another.

We, (your name) and (other's name), share our multiple feelings with others.

Reciprocal Affirmations

I, (your name), share my multiple feelings with you.

You, (other's name), share your multiple feelings with me.

We, (your name) and (other's name), share our multiple feelings with each other.

(Your name) and (other's name) share their multiple feelings with each other.

Much of what we do may be motivated by attempts to please others. But our greatest satisfaction and our most productive work come from pleasing ourselves. If we push ourselves beyond our comfort zone to please others, we are liable to feel unappreciated and inadequate when we don't get enthusiastic praise. Burnout becomes a real risk.

When we are doing things we enjoy, our whole being is cooperating and our product has an attractive wholeness about it. No matter what we think others want, they will ultimately appreciate and praise us most when we're doing what is meaningful and pleasurable to us.

Personal Affirmations

I, (your name), am praised for doing what I enjoy.

You, (your name), are praised for doing what you enjoy.

(Your name) is praised for doing what she/he enjoys.

We, (your name) and (other's name), are praised for doing what we enjoy.

Reciprocal Affirmations

I, (your name), receive your praise for doing what I enjoy.

You, (other's name), receive my praise for doing what you enjoy.

We, (your name) and (other's name), receive each other's praise for doing what we enjoy.

(Your name) and (other's name) receive each other's praise for doing what they enjoy.

In our relationships we like to agree on as many things as possible. But if we insist on agreement in every little thing, we lose one of the basic satisfactions of a relationship — having someone different from ourselves affirm our choices.

Differences in matters of personal style, the pace of talking, sensory pleasures or information processing may be a source of friction in our relationships. But we need to give others and ourselves the freedom to reach decisions on our own and find agreement in our own fashion. With a broader base of complementary experiences, rather than duplication or imitation, our agreements will be deeper and more satisfying.

Personal Affirmations

I, (your name), don't insist on agreement with others.
You, (your name), don't insist on agreement with others.
(Your name) doesn't insist on agreement with others.
We, (your name) and (other's name), don't insist on agreement with others.

Reciprocal Affirmations

I, (your name), don't insist on agreement from you.
You, (other's name), don't insist on agreement from me.
We, (your name) and (other's name), don't insist on agreement with each other.
(Your name) and (other's name) don't insist on agreement with each other.

Anger and frustration are a very real part of everyone's life. And we frequently vent on those closest to us. Often we transfer our anger or frustration to something the other has or hasn't done, rather than keep it where it is. How can we let it out without taking it out on those close to us?

"I'm angry. I'm frustrated. I'm really angry! I'm very frustrated!" Just saying it over and over can help us release it without provoking or blaming the other. Remember, you own your anger and frustration. When you take it out on someone else, they won't be the source of empathy and support they might have been.

Personal Affirmations

I, (your name), own my anger and frustration.
You, (your name), own your anger and frustration.
(Your name) owns her/his anger and frustration.
We, (your name) and (other's name), each own our
    own anger and frustration.

Reciprocal Affirmations

I, (your name), own my own anger and frustration.
You, (other's name), own your own anger and frustra-
    tion.
We, (your name) and (other's name), each own our
    own anger and frustration.
(Your name) and (other's name) each own their own
    anger and frustration.

When we make a decision with someone else, we must first be honest with ourselves about what we want and don't want. If we set our mind on getting what we know is more than the other is comfortable with, we are unlikely to find agreement. On the other hand, if we set our mind on settling quickly for less than we are comfortable with in order to avoid conflict, we're asking for disappointment and resentment.

What aspects of the decision are most important to me? What aspects are least important? I can stand fast on the important ones and negotiate on the unimportant ones, but only if I take time to know my own mind.

Personal Affirmations

I, (your name), know my own mind in joint decisions.

You, (your name), know your own mind in joint decisions.

(Your name) knows her/his own mind in joint decisions.

We, (your name) and (other's name), each know our own mind in joint decisions.

Reciprocal Affirmations

I, (your name), know my own mind in joint decisions.

You, (other's name), know your own mind in joint decisions.

We, (your name) and (other's name), each know our own mind in joint decisions.

(Your name) and (other's name) each know their own mind in joint decisions.

When we're preoccupied with a situation or extremely busy, we may be forgetful or have a series of accidents, hopefully small ones. What's behind this?

Our mind is so busy with the preoccupation or multitude of details that it can't or doesn't give enough attention to our present situation. This causes us to forget what we're doing or not to perform well, leading to an accident.

Accident-proneness and forgetfulness can be signals given to us by our body to slow down or stop being preoccupied. If our body has recognized the signs, it's likely others have too. We can improve our relationships and our lives by listening to our body's warning signs.

Personal Affirmations

I, (your name), heed my body's warning signs.

You, (your name), heed your body's warning signs.

(Your name) heeds her/his body's warning signs.

We, (your name) and (other's name), heed our bodies' warning signs.

Reciprocal Affirmations

I, (your name), heed my body's warning signs.

You, (other's name), heed your body's warning signs.

We, (your name) and (other's name), each heed our bodies' warning signs.

(Your name) and (other's name) each heed their bodies' warning signs.

We can start each day with a fresh, open attitude, ready to make the best of whatever it brings. But to do this we need to live consciously. The past runs our lives through the subconscious. If we move through our day at a low level of conscious awareness, we'll be controlled by habits, expectations and attitudes from the past.

We need to focus consciously on our unlimited potential for creative expression, spiritual growth and satisfying relationships. This awareness helps us build a positive attitude that enriches our day and all our interactions.

Personal Affirmations

I, (your name), increase conscious awareness in my life.

You, (your name), increase conscious awareness in your life.

(Your name) increases conscious awareness in her/his life.

We, (your name) and (other's name), increase conscious awareness in our lives.

Reciprocal Affirmations

I, (your name), increase conscious awareness in my life.

You, (other's name), increase conscious awareness in your life.

We, (your name) and (other's name), increase conscious awareness in our lives.

(Your name) and (other's name) increase conscious awareness in their lives.

We can't get inside another's mind. We do best not to try. When we try to second-guess another's thoughts and motivations, we will be wrong as often as right. Even if we guess correctly, we're taking on responsibility that is not ours. We encourage irrationality and in effect deny the other's responsibiity to take conscious control of their own lives and express themselves clearly to us.

Instead we need to go slowly when we're listening and not assume we understand until we have listened with patience and respect.

Personal Affirmations

I, (your name), listen patiently and respectfully.

You, (your name), listen patiently and respectfully.

(Your name) listens patiently and respectfully.

We, (your name) and (other's name), listen patiently and respectfully.

Reciprocal Affirmations

I, (your name), listen to you patiently and respectfully.

You, (other's name), listen to me patiently and respectfully.

We, (your name) and (other's name), listen to each other patiently and respectfully.

(Your name) and (other's name) listen to each other patiently and respectfully.

In our relationships, we often have a private agenda of what we want for ourselves, what we want the other to do and how we want to change the relationship.

A time of sharing personal goals and then developing joint goals for the relationship can be very helpful. It can clarify which goals are realistic and which may be unachievable, beyond our control or none of our business. We can let go of secret goals when we have common ones.

Finding common goals builds better understanding and mutual trust. It infuses new energy. Some possible goals are to make shared decisions weekly, take long vacations or give affectionate touching daily.

Personal Affirmations

I, (your name), share my goals for my relationship.

You, (your name), share your goals for your relationship.

(Your name) shares her/his goals for her/his relationship.

We, (your name) and (other's name), share our goals for our relationship.

Reciprocal Affirmations

I, (your name), share my goals for our relationship.

You, (other's name), share your goals for our relationship.

We, (your name) and (other's name), share our goals for our relationship.

(Your name) and (other's name) share their goals for their relationship.

In our past relationships we may have picked up negative messages that affect new relationships. In our family of origin we may have taken blame for others' failures or felt inadequate or undeserving of real happiness. In our new relationships we may unconsciously assume we must work extra hard to deserve love, that we are responsible if anything goes wrong or that happiness is not for us.

Today we can let go of these misinterpretations of our past. Much that happened was beyond our understanding as children, and most negative messages we absorbed were wrong. Today I am entitled to be loved unconditionally, to love freely, and to have fun. I can freely discard old patterns for new.

Personal Affirmations

I, (your name), am free to have relationships that feel good to me.

You, (your name), are free to have relationships that feel good to you.

(Your name) is free to have relationships that feel good to her/him.

We, (your name) and (other's name), are free to have relationships that feel good to us.

Reciprocal Affirmations

I, (your name), am free to have a relationship that feels good to me.

You, (other's name), are free to have a relationship that feels good to you.

We, (your name) and (other's name), are free to have a relationship that feels good to us.

(Your name) and (other's name) are free to have a relationship that feels good to them.

Sometimes we feel we're in a relationship rut. It's not that the relationship is bad, it's just that things are too routine. The excitement is gone. We would like to recapture the lost joy, anticipation and excitement.

One way to pull out of the rut is to examine our routines and habits and then change them. We can put variety or spice back into our interactions by allowing more of the unexpected. We can do it for our personal routines and for routines we share. By examining and changing our routines, we can make everyday interactions more exciting.

Personal Affirmations

I, (your name), keep my relationships fresh by varying my routines.

You, (your name), keep your relationships fresh by varying your routines.

(Your name) keeps her/his relationships fresh by varying her/his routines.

We, (your name) and (other's name), keep our relationships fresh by varying our routines.

Reciprocal Affirmations

I, (your name), keep our relationship fresh by varying my routines.

You, (other's name), keep our relationship fresh by varying your routines.

We, (your name) and (other's name), keep our relationship fresh by varying our routines.

(Your name) and (other's name) keep their relationship fresh by varying their routines.

Each of us has a unique path to follow. None can pass judgment on another. We cannot know each other's deepest needs and wants, nor should we want to. If we judge those we love, we are loving conditionally. That burden hurts us both.

Good judgment serves us well to select information useful to us, to choose words and actions that reflect our higher selves and to discover what relationships are right for us and need cultivation.

But our judgment doesn't serve us well when we use it to attack others or condemn them. In our relationships we must set aside our judgment, show compassion and give unconditional love.

Personal Affirmations

I, (your name), love without conditions.
You, (your name), love without conditions.
(Your name) loves without condtions.
We, (your name) and (other's name), love without conditions.

Reciprocal Affirmations

I, (your name), love you unconditionally.
You, (other's name), love me unconditionally.
We, (your name) and (other's name), love each other unconditionally.
(Your name) and (other's name) love each other unconditionally.

Laughing is a physical release of tension. Even a smile is a small release of tension. That's one of the reasons we feel better when we laugh.

Laughing is primarily a social phenomenon. Although it happens, we don't often laugh by ourselves. Usually we laugh when others are around. We relate to others when we laugh together. We appreciate the same humor. We draw closer as human beings because we share the same feelings. We improve our relationships when we find things to laugh about together.

Personal Affirmations

I, (your name), find things to laugh about with others.

You, (your name), find things to laugh about with others.

(Your name) finds things to laugh about with others.

We, (your name) and (other's name), find things to laugh about with others.

Reciprocal Affirmations

I, (your name), find things to laugh about with you.

You, (other's name), find things to laugh about with me.

We, (your name) and (other's name), find things to laugh about with each other.

(Your name) and (other's name) find things to laugh about with each other.

Do we sometimes feel another doesn't appreciate all we've done or that we've cared enough to take on another chore? Our reaction may be to get mad and decide the other is a "worthless ingrate."

It's important to realize that most of us feel unappreciated from time to time. At these times we need to express our feelings and say, "I'm feeling unappreciated." Regardless of the response we get from the other, we have acknowledged to ourselves that our feelings count and that we are allowed to express them. If the other gives an appreciative response, we can consider it a bonus reinforcing our self-appreciation.

Personal Affirmations

I, (your name), express my feelings when I feel unappreciated.

You, (your name), express your feelings when you feel unappreciated.

(Your name) expresses her/his feelings when she/he feels unappreciated.

We, (your name) and (other's name), each express our feelings when we feel unappreciated.

Reciprocal Affirmations

I, (your name), express my feelings when I feel unappreciated by you.

You, (other's name), express your feelings when you feel unappreciated by me.

We, (your name) and (other's name), express our feelings when we feel unappreciated by the other.

(Your name) and (other's name) express their feelings when they feel unappreciated by the other.

One of the most pleasurable ways we communicate with our partner in an intimate relationship is through sex. If we feel any dissatisfaction with our sex life, we need to be honest about our feelings and sexual preferences and communicate them to our partner.

Honesty in sexual matters will at a minimum make us feel good about ourselves because it acknowledges that our feelings and preferences count and we have a right to satisfy them. Such honesty may also result in our partner helping us get the satisfaction we want.

Personal Affirmations
I, (your name), am honest with my sex partner.
You, (your name), are honest with your sex partner.
(Your name) is honest with her/his sex partner.
We, (your name) and (other's name), are honest with each other about sex.

Reciprocal Affirmations
I, (your name), am honest with you about sex.
You, (other's name), are honest with me about sex.
We, (your name) and (other's name), are honest with each other about sex.
(Your name) and (other's name) are honest with each other about sex.

When we have persistent problems in our relationships, we may become advice shoppers, collectors of potential solutions and perennial seekers. We may try one suggestion for a time and then flip to another when the first doesn't get quick results. We may blame our advisers for lack of success.

The real solutions to our problems come from within. Even if someone offers the right solution for us, it won't work until we make it our own. We need belief and commitment to make a solution work. Good listening to well-meant advice is useful, but we must view it only as offering options. We must make the choice and we must live with the results.

Personal Affirmations

I, (your name), hear advice as only part of my problem-solving.

You, (your name), hear advice as only part of your problem-solving.

(Your name) hears advice as only part of her/his problem-solving.

We, (your name) and (other's name), hear advice as only part of our problem-solving.

Reciprocal Affirmations

I, (your name), hear your advice as only part of my problem-solving.

You, (other's name), hear my advice as only part of your problem-solving.

We, (your name) and (other's name), hear each other's advice as only part of our problem-solving.

(Your name) and (other's name) hear each other's advice as only part of their problem-solving.

Impatience affects our relationship when we assume another is slow, stupid or uncaring because they don't respond instantly. "Pick up your napkin. Pick up your napkin! PICK UP YOUR NAPKIN! I'VE ASKED YOU THREE TIMES!" Sometimes we expect another to react faster than they can or are comfortable with.

We need to give others the opportunity not only to hear what we say, but to think about it, decide for themselves if they want to cooperate and then send a message from their brain to the part of their body that will respond. Being patient shows respect for the other's right to respond in their own way in their own time.

Personal Affirmations

I, (your name), am patient.

You, (your name), are patient.

(Your name) is patient.

We, (your name) and (other's name), are patient with others.

Reciprocal Affirmations

I, (your name), am patient with you.

You, (other's name), are patient with me.

We, (your name) and (other's name), are patient with each other.

(Your name) and (other's name) are patient with each other.

We're in danger of getting entangled in the problems of those we care about most. I need my energy to run my life and solve my own problems.

I can show others I care about them by empathizing with them when they have problems. But it's ineffective for me to worry for or with them or to try to control the way they deal with their problems. To do so interferes or meddles in the other's life.

Personal Affirmations

I, (your name), mind my own business.

You, (your name), mind your own business.

(Your name) minds her/his own business.

We, (your name) and (other's name), mind our own business.

Reciprocal Affirmations

I, (your name), stay out of your business.

You, (other's name), stay out of my business.

We, (your name) and (other's name), stay out of each other's business.

(Your name) and (other's name) mind their own business.

We can cultivate and maintain the fun and spontaneity in even our most serious relationships by giving more rein to our natural curiosity. In our drive to know the other, to learn, to understand, to decide, we often forget that life and love are even more about experiencing and enjoying.

A new hat, a different turn of phrase, an unusual laugh or a new dietary preference does not have to be seen as a disruption to our expectations or a matter for analysis or understanding. Instead we need to cultivate our ability to treat these as opportunities to enjoy the other's unfettered individuality as it enriches our life.

Personal Affirmations

I, (your name), enjoy my natural curiosity.
You, (your name), enjoy your natural curiosity.
(Your name) enjoys her/his natural curiosity.
We, (your name) and (other's name), enjoy our natural curiosity.

Reciprocal Affirmations

I, (your name), enjoy my natural curiosity about you.
You, (other's name), enjoy your natural curiosity about me.
We, (your name) and (other's name), enjoy our natural curiosity about each other.
(Your name) and (other's name) enjoy their natural curiosity about each other.

Sometimes we let ourselves get into a rut of the familiar. We're more comfortable if nothing rocks our boat. We feel in control if we know everything will be familiar. We're afraid that, if we encounter new or different things, we will have to re-evaluate everything in our lives. And we fear that if we encounter different people, they will judge us critically.

What a joy it is to just enjoy new and different things without judging, to be curious without self-doubt about the way we do things, to appreciate individuality without being critical of ourselves or the other. We can enjoy the differences.

Personal Affirmations

I, (your name), enjoy new experiences with enthusiasm.

You, (your name), enjoy new experiences with enthusiasm.

(Your name) enjoys new experiences with enthusiasm.

We, (your name) and (other's name), enjoy new experiences with enthusiasm.

Reciprocal Affirmations

I, (your name), enjoy new experiences with enthusiasm.

You, (other's name), enjoy new experiences with enthusiasm.

We, (your name) and (other's name), enjoy new experiences with enthusiasm.

(Your name) and (other's name) enjoy new experiences with enthusiasm.

The words I choose when talking to myself or others are important. Our brains receive everything we hear and on some level the words make an impression. This is true whether I'm talking or listening. Words not only reflect my general view of life — positive or negative, optimistic or pessimistic, the glass half full or half empty — but they also help form it.

Sarcasm and other forms of put-down are especially bad. These joking or half-serious witticisms can devastate the listener. The listener's brain doesn't always see the humor and when it does, humor is only part of the message. The other part is literal.

Personal Affirmations

I, (your name), choose my words carefully.

You, (your name), choose your words carefully.

(Your name) chooses her/his words carefully.

We, (your name) and (other's name), choose our words carefully.

Reciprocal Affirmations

I, (your name), choose my words carefully.

You, (other's name), choose your words carefully.

We, (your name) and (other's name), choose our words carefully.

(Your name) and (other's name) choose their words carefully.

Are we proud of our sense of color and style? Do we use it to help our partner dress well? Do we buy their clothes for them? Or do we tell them, either with or without their asking, what they should wear today? What have we done to their self-esteem by implying they aren't capable of dressing themselves without our help?

We have no business making any decisions for another. Whether it's what clothes to wear, what job to take or how to spend their leisure time, it's none of our business. Even if we think we could do better, we need to keep it to ourselves.

Personal Affirmations

I, (your name), let others make their own decisions.
You, (your name), let others make their own decisions.
(Your name) lets others make their own decisions.
*We, (your name) and (other's name), let others make
    their own decisions.*

Reciprocal Affirmations

I, (your name), let you make your own decisions.
You, (other's name), let me make my own decisions.
*We, (your name) and (other's name), let each other
    make their own decisions.*
*(Your name) and (other's name) each let the other
    make their own decisions.*

Experience is a great teacher. Our communication with others is especially open to learning by experience. We learn what works and what doesn't. We try new behaviors in similar or different situations. We grow.

Our sexual communication is similar to our other types of communication. We can continually improve it through experience, and that increases our sexual pleasure. We need to be open to learning and growth and willing to make changes, even small ones.

Personal Affirmations

I, (your name), improve my sexual communication
    and pleasure.

You, (your name), improve your sexual communica-
    tion and pleasure.

(Your name) improves her/his sexual communication
    and pleasure.

We, (your name) and (other's name), improve our
    sexual communication and pleasure.

Reciprocal Affirmations

I, (your name), improve my sexual communication
    and pleasure.

You, (other's name), improve your sexual communica-
    tion and pleasure.

We, (your name) and (other's name), improve our
    sexual communication and pleasure.

(Your name) and (other's name) improve their sexual
    communication and pleasure.

Many of us have experienced great pain from a failed relationship or an event such as the death of a loved one. We feel a need to talk about it to anyone who will listen. How much can we talk about it without unduly burdening the other or jeopardizing our relationship?

It's always okay to talk about what is getting in the way of our present relationship. "I'm sorry I reacted like that. It reminded me of when my former spouse . . ." But when we go into details beyond those that relate to our present relationship, we had best stop. The rest is for us to work out on our own, with a professional or in a self-help group.

Personal Affirmations

I, (your name), work out my past pain without burdening others.

You, (your name), work out your past pain without burdening others.

(Your name) works out her/his past pain without burdening others.

We, (your name) and (other's name), work out our past pain without burdening others.

Reciprocal Affirmations

I, (your name), work out my past pain without burdening you.

You, (other's name), work out your past pain without burdening me.

We, (your name) and (other's name), work out our past pain without burdening each other.

(Your name) and (other's name) work out their past pain without burdening each other.

Sometimes we think our partner is behaving inappropriately toward our children or friends. We tell them how to behave, we apologize for their actions or we try to make up for their behavior. In each of these cases, we aren't letting them have a direct relationship with our children or friends.

Everyone has needs and is entitled to a direct relationship with others. A father and mother each have separate direct relationships with their children. We need to give them space to make their own mistakes and have their own direct relationships.

Personal Affirmations

I, (your name), allow others space for their own direct relationships.

You, (your name), allow others space for their own direct relationships.

(Your name) allows others space for their own direct relationships.

We, (your name) and (other's name), allow others space for their own direct relationships.

Reciprocal Affirmations

I, (your name), allow you space for your own direct relationships.

You, (other's name), allow me space for my own direct relationships.

We, (your name) and (other's name), allow each other space for our own direct relationships.

(Your name) and (other's name) allow each other space for their own direct relationships.

In our eagerness to be connected to another, we may immerse ourselves in admiring and pleasing another to the exclusion of our other responsibilities. Then when we feel there is a commitment, we may turn back to the rest of our lives and forget that a relationship takes regular positive input to maintain a positive tone.

If we assume we have found the perfect mate or best friend, we still cannot take for granted that our relationship will be perfect. And without continuing commitment from us, we may meet the inevitable imperfections that do develop with blame and manipulation rather than with the positive input a good relationship deserves.

Personal Affirmations

I, (your name), take responsibility for the positive tone of my relationships.

You, (your name), take responsibility for the positive tone of your relationships.

(Your name) takes responsibility for the positive tone of her/his relationships.

We, (your name) and (other's name), take responsibility for the positive tone of our relationships.

Reciprocal Affirmations

I, (your name), take responsibility for the positive tone of our relationship.

You, (other's name), take responsibility for the positive tone of our relationship.

We, (your name) and (other's name), take responsibility for the positive tone of our relationship.

(Your name) and (other's name) take responsibility for the positive tone of their relationship.

When we're feeling happy, it's easy to smile. Happiness creates an impulse to smile. But we may not realize that the reverse is also true. When we smile, it's easier to be happy. Smiling creates an impulse to feel happy.

This is simply an example of the interaction of mind and body, a sophisticated feedback loop that operates constantly. If we want to improve the quality of our relationships, something as simple as adding three more smiles a day to our life can stimulate new, more congenial responses from others.

Personal Affirmations

I, (your name), add three smiles to my day.
You, (your name), add three smiles to your day.
(Your name) adds three smiles to her/his day.
We, (your name) and (other's name), each add three smiles to our day.

Reciprocal Affirmations

I, (your name), smile at you more often today.
You, (other's name), smile at me more often today.
We, (your name) and (other's name), smile at each other more often today.
(Your name) and (other's name) smile at each other more often today.

Feelings. What am I feeling right now? Am I willing to tell the person next to me what I'm feeling?

If I'm not sure what I'm feeling, I may be hiding my feelings from myself. I may be afraid to express my feelings or identify them, or I may hold them in. These only create distance, coolness or bottled-up emotions.

Sharing my feelings with others is healthy, lets out my emotions and feels good. It may seem scary at first. But I can't expect others to know my needs and desires unless I share my feelings. My happiness can only come when I get my feelings out in constructive ways.

Personal Affirmations

I, (your name), open up and share my feelings.

You, (your name), open up and share your feelings.

(Your name) opens up and shares her/his feelings.

We, (your name) and (other's name), open up and share our feelings.

Reciprocal Affirmations

I, (your name), open up and share my feelings with you.

You, (other's name), open up and share your feelings with me.

We, (your name) and (other's name), open up and share our feelings with each other.

(Your name) and (other's name) open up and share their feelings with each other.

When we feel uneasy about a relationship, we may be tempted to spend so much effort on it that we jeopardize our own health. We may stay up late worrying or arguing. We may skip preparing meals or eating them. We may ignore signs of exhaustion, thirst, depression or increased susceptibility to disease. We may dress inappropriately for the weather. We may handle tools, equipment or cars with less care.

Our first duty is to ourselves. Temporary setbacks in relationshps are most often exactly that — temporary. If we do nothing, they will resolve themselves. Even if a relationship is deteriorating, taking risks with our health will make us less able to deal with it.

Personal Affirmations
I, (your name), set high priority on my health.
You, (your name), set high priority on your health.
(Your name) sets high priority on her/his health.
*We, (your name) and (other's name), each set high
    priority on our own health.*

Reciprocal Affirmations
I, (your name), set high priority on my health.
You, (other's name), set high priority on your health.
*We, (your name) and (other's name), each set high
    priority on our own health.*
*(Your name) and (other's name) set high priority on
    their own health.*

Sometimes a change in our partner's life gives us a rude awakening. We may have reached a comfortable plateau where we can see far out in front of us, and then something in the other's life interferes. It may be the death of a parent, a career change, sudden dissatisfaction with the daily routine or something else.

These changes remind us that the only life we have any control over is our own. If we want to avoid being at the mercy of shifting winds on the sea of life, we must fine-tune our own attitudes so we can adjust quickly to maintain our balance and direction. Then, when our partner needs us, we can be supportive, not resentful.

Personal Affirmations

I, (your name), fine-tune my navigational skills for life.

You, (your name), fine-tune your navigational skills for life.

(Your name) fine-tunes her/his navigational skills for life.

We, (your name) and (other's name), fine-tune our navigational skills for life.

Reciprocal Affirmations

I, (your name), fine-tune my navigational skills for life.

You, (other's name), fine-tune your navigational skills for life.

We, (your name) and (other's name), fine-tune our navigational skills for life.

(Your name) and (other's name) fine-tune their navigational skills for life.

We've heard that to be a healthy person and have a healthy relationship we must put ourselves first. Do we give, give, give to the other without thought of our own needs? Do we strive to get everything exactly as the other likes it and then harbor resentment because we're unappreciated? What does it mean to put ourselves first?

Putting ourselves first begins on the emotional level. We have to put our emotional needs first. Once we are together emotionally, we can offer emotional support to others as long as we don't do things that bump us down to second place. Once our emotions are in order, our behavior and interactions will have a healthy flow.

Personal Affirmations

I, (your name), take care of my emotional needs first.
You, (your name), take care of your emotional needs first.
(Your name) takes care of her/his emotional needs first.
We, (your name) and (other's name), each take care of our own emotional needs first.

Reciprocal Affirmations

I, (your name), take care of my emotional needs first.
You, (other's name), take care of your emotional needs first.
We, (your name) and (other's name), each take care of our own emotional needs first.
(Your name) and (other's name) each take care of their own emotional needs first.

The need to love and be loved is basic. It comes right behind the three necessities of food, shelter and clothing. Since love is such an important aspect of human life, it's okay to devote a lot of energy to the relationships that sustain it.

Sometimes we put the quest for luxury items — a stylish pocketbook, a new VCR or car — ahead of time with our children or spouse working on our relationships. We need to consider what things are really important to us and act accordingly.

Personal Affirmations

I, (your name), give high priority to my relationships.

You, (your name), give high priority to your relationships.

(Your name) gives high priority to her/his relationships.

We, (your name) and (other's name), give high priority to our relationships.

Reciprocal Affirmations

I, (your name), give high priority to our relationship.

You, (other's name), give high priority to our relationship.

We, (your name) and (other's name), give high priority to our relationship.

(Your name) and (other's name) give high priority to their relationship.

We all want to achieve inner peace. One major tool to help us achieve that goal is acceptance. Acceptance is loving ourselves for who we are as we are, loving others as they are and not trying to change those things we can't control — such as other people.

Home is a good place to practice acceptance. We and the other people in our home will achieve more inner peace if we start being accepting of each other. When our home is an accepting place, we will have the strength to expand our acceptance to other areas of our lives.

Personal Affirmations

I, (your name), begin with acceptance at home.
You, (your name), begin with acceptance at home.
(Your name) begins with acceptance at home.
We, (your name) and (other's name), begin with acceptance at home.

Reciprocal Affirmations

I, (your name), begin with accepting you at home.
You, (other's name), begin with accepting me at home.
We, (your name) and (other's name), begin with accepting each other at home.
(Your name) and (other's name) begin with accepting each other at home.

If another makes financial contributions to our life, we may maintain an attitude of continual sacrifice. We may think that always spending a little less than we want will keep us grateful. Our partner may even shame us into that behavior by saying, "You spend whatever you want, while I pay the bills."

But if our relationship involves a division of labor — delegating individual functions to one another — our contributions are equivalent regardless of who earns the money. If we value our own time and effort, we can appreciate that our decision to be financially dependent doesn't compromise our independence as a person.

Personal Affirmations
Financial dependence doesn't compromise my personal value.
(Your name), financial dependence doesn't compromise your personal value.
Financial dependence doesn't compromise (your name)'s personal value.
Financial dependence doesn't compromise the personal value of either of us.

Reciprocal Affirmations
Financial dependence doesn't compromise my personal value.
Financial dependence doesn't compromise your personal value.
Financial dependence doesn't compromise the personal value of either of us.
Financial dependence doesn't compromise (your name) or (other's name)'s personal value.

We seek to be generous in our relationships by giving of ourselves and our possessions. But sometimes our generosity goes unappreciated. We may feel bitter, angry or resentful. We may determine to try harder and harder until our generosity gets noticed.

This becomes a trap that pulls us away from our true selves and makes us less and less capable of true generosity. If we care about whether our generosity is appreciated, then most likely we don't appreciate it ourselves. If we can't give something without demanding an emotional payoff, we have pushed ourselves too far.

Personal Affirmations

I, (your name), am generous with no strings attached.

You, (your name), are generous with no strings attached.

(Your name) is generous with no strings attached.

We, (your name) and (other's name), are generous with no strings attached.

Reciprocal Affirmations

I, (your name), am generous with no strings attached.

You, (other's name), are generous with no strings attached.

We, (your name) and (other's name), are generous with no strings attached.

(Your name) and (other's name) are generous with no strings attached.

Sometimes in a sexual relationship, we try to be wholly spontaneous and responsive. We seek to enjoy a total departure from our otherwise structured, goal-oriented existence. But then we may be painfully disappointed and feel manipulated, unappreciated or unsatisfied when a sexual encounter doesn't meet our desires.

Our sexual satisfaction is our responsibility. But we don't have to sacrifice our spontaneity to get it. The key is to get rid of goals that require specific input from our partner and develop goals over which we have total personal control. These might be enjoying the other's physical presence, enjoying our own arousal response to the other or enjoying our sense of spiritual union.

Personal Affirmations

I, (your name), enjoy sexual spontaneity without forfeiting satisfaction.

You, (your name), enjoy sexual spontaneity without forfeiting satisfaction.

(Your name) enjoys sexual spontaneity without forfeiting satisfaction.

We, (your name) and (other's name), enjoy sexual spontaneity without forfeiting satisfaction.

Reciprocal Affirmations

I, (your name), enjoy sexual spontaneity without forfeiting satisfaction.

You, (other's name), enjoy sexual spontaneity without forfeiting satisfaction.

We, (your name) and (other's name), enjoy sexual spontaneity without forfeiting satisfaction.

(Your name) and (other's name) enjoy sexual spontaneity without forfeiting satisfaction.

Some of us wish we had more or deeper friendships with people of our own sex. Our self-image is often to blame. If we define ourselves by our attractiveness to the opposite sex, we're constantly comparing ourselves to others and fear we'll come up short or we seek constant praise and fear rejection.

We need to affirm our inherent value independent of our sexual attractiveness. We can acknowledge it and own it without any need to test it or prove it in our same-sex relationships.

Personal Affirmations

My same-sex friends like me, (your name), just for who I am.

(Your name), your same-sex friends like you just for who you are.

(Your name)'s same-sex friends like her/him just for who she/he is.

Our same-sex friends like each of us just for who we are.

Reciprocal Affirmations

My same-sex friends like me, (your name), just for who I am.

Your same-sex friends like you, (other's name), just for who you are.

Our same-sex friends like each of us just for who we are.

(Your name) and (other's name)'s same-sex friends like them for who they are.

We value sharing highly in a relationship. What does that really mean? As children we may have been told to "share" when we were really being told to give up what we wanted. This misnomer encourages an attitude of scarcity, resentment and helplessness. We imagine that to have what we want we must deprive someone else, and conversely, that to please another we must deprive ourselves.

Sharing isn't the painful task of giving up what we want. We all share in the abundance of the universe. Sharing is the creation of more for all by the giving to another of ourselves, our possessions, or anything else we are comfortable giving.

Personal Affirmations

I, (your name), share with an attitude of abundance.

You, (your name), share with an attitude of abundance.

(Your name) shares with an attitude of abundance.

We, (your name) and (other's name), share with an attitude of abundance.

Reciprocal Affirmations

I, (your name), share with you with an attitude of abundance.

You, (other's name), share with me with an attitude of abundance.

We, (your name) and (other's name), share with each other with an attitude of abundance.

(Your name) and (other's name) share with each other with an attitude of abundance.

In a mobile society with each nuclear family having its own home, work and places for education and recreation, there is little opportunity to form lasting friendships with older people. How many people even ten years older than ourselves do we have to call friends?

Perhaps we never had a chance to chat with a grandparent or we don't feel comfortable in friendly conversation with a parent. We can build enriching friendships now with the elderly shopkeeper, the live-in parent of a friend, an elderly teacher in our children's school or a neighbor. Our heightened sense of perspective, of continuity, of belonging to something larger than ourselves and of affirming our own youth and opportunity is worth the effort.

Personal Affirmations

I, (your name), get along with older people.
You, (your name), get along with older people.
(Your name) gets along with older people.
We, (your name) and (other's name), get along with older people.

Reciprocal Affirmations

I, (your name), get along with older people.
You, (other's name), get along with older people.
We, (your name) and (other's name), get along with older people.
(Your name) and (other's name) get along with older people.

If we find our relationships unsatisfactory, we need to assess our relationship with ourselves. If that is weak, others are hard to sustain. Perhaps we don't think enough of ourselves. Perhaps we neglect our feelings. Perhaps we don't spend enough time with ourselves or we deny ourselves simple pleasures like a good book or a relaxing bath. Perhaps we carry grudges against ourselves for past wrongs.

If we don't feel in touch with ourselves — the person we care most about and for whom we are most responsible — we will find it hard to stay in touch with and care about others. If we love and care for ourselves, other relationships will prove more satisfactory.

Personal Affirmations

I, (your name), am building a good relationship with myself.

You, (your name), are building a good relationship with yourself.

(Your name) is building a good relationship with herself/himself.

We, (your name) and (other's name), are building good relationships with ourselves.

Reciprocal Affirmations

I, (your name), am building a good relationship with myself.

You, (other's name), are building a good relationship with yourself.

We, (your name) and (other's name), are building good relationships with ourselves.

(Your name) and (other's name) are building good relationships with themselves.

Arguments mark every relationship. Sometimes they get very intense. We've all argued with people who don't give up the argument, who won't let us change the subject even for an entire social evening or who just won't let go. How do we get out of the situation without losing a friend?

For some reason the other's ego and sense of self-worth are wrapped up in convincing us or winning the argument. We need to realize it's the other's problem. We don't need to capitulate or let them win. All we need do is say we disagree and walk away from the argument, literally if necessary.

Personal Affirmations

I, (your name), feel free to walk away from an argument.

You, (your name), feel free to walk away from an argument.

(Your name) feels free to walk away from an argument.

We, (your name) and (other's name), each feel free to walk away from an argument.

Reciprocal Affirmations

I, (your name), feel free to walk away from arguing with you.

You, (other's name), feel free to walk away from arguing with me.

We, (your name) and (other's name), each feel free to walk away from arguing with the other.

(Your name) and (other's name) each feel free to walk away from arguing with each other.

At one time or another, we have all felt alone, as if no one understands us or our problems. Sometimes we are just plain lonely, with no one to love or share life's daily pleasures and tribulations.

Sharing with another, relating to their humanity, is the cure to loneliness or feeling alone. The other need not be the love of your life, but could be a friend, co-worker or casual acquaintance. It's the act of sharing, of relating, that lets us feel connected.

Personal Affirmations
I, (your name), reach out and connect with others.
You, (your name), reach out and connect with others.
(Your name) reaches out and connects with others.
We, (your name) and (other's name), reach out and connect with others.

Reciprocal Affirmations
I, (your name), reach out and connect with you.
You, (other's name), reach out and connect with me.
We, (your name) and (other's name), reach out and connect with each other.
(Your name) and (other's name) reach out and connect with each other.

A relationship can stagnate and go sour if we don't take time to emphasize and enjoy its good points and strengths. Finding events to celebrate helps reinforce the growth in the relationship. We can celebrate any event or new stage in a relationship — when we met, when we wed, when we moved to our favorite living space, when a child was born, when we paid off a debt.

If an important event did not have a specific date, we can designate one and celebrate it together. We can have weekly and monthly as well as yearly anniversaries. It's all right to fill our lives with uplifting celebration.

Personal Affirmations

I, (your name), find events to celebrate in my relationships.

You, (your name), find events to celebrate in your relationships.

(Your name) finds events to celebrate in her/his relationships.

We, (your name) and (other's name), find events to celebrate in our relationships.

Reciprocal Affirmations

I, (your name), find events to celebrate in our relationship.

You, (other's name), find events to celebrate in our relationship.

We, (your name) and (other's name), find events to celebrate in our relationship.

(Your name) and (other's name) find events to celebrate in their relationship.

We are creatures of habit in our relationships. Our habits of interaction are largely responsible for the way we feel. If we aren't happy with a relationship, we can't count on it getting better unless we're open to changing our habits. What's more, no relationship stays the same, waiting for us to decide to change. Feelings and reactions change with time, so our habits of interaction affect the relationship differently. And habits get more entrenched the longer we practice them, so a bad situation gets worse.

Being creatures of habit isn't as great a limitation as we may think. We can consciously change habits. And we can learn any new habits we want with patience and practice.

Personal Affirmations
I, (your name), change my habits for the better.
You, (your name), change your habits for the better.
(Your name) changes her/his habits for the better.
We, (your name) and (other's name), change our habits for the better.

Reciprocal Affirmations
I, (your name), change my habits for the better.
You, (other's name), change your habits for the better.
We, (your name) and (other's name), change our habits for the better.
(Your name) and (other's name) change their habits for the better.

We find it easier to get along with others when we're doing fun things together. We may be waiting until we have more time or money for a vacation, dining out, a concert or a show, a club membership or a ski weekend. We may have to wait a long time for these things.

Meanwhile, we can change our thinking to find shorter and cheaper activities that give us fun things to do together. We can take a walk, play a board game, share each other's favorite TV show, rent an old video we both liked as kids, cook together, window-shop together, read the same book or exchange limericks. Small things can have great impact.

Personal Affirmations

I, (your name), look for fun little things to do.

You, (your name), look for fun little things to do.

(Your name) looks for fun little things to do.

We, (your name) and (other's name), look for fun little things to do.

Reciprocal Affirmations

I, (your name), look for fun little things to do with you.

You, (other's name), look for fun little things to do with me.

We, (your name) and (other's name), look for fun little things to do together.

(Your name) and (other's name) look for fun little things to do together.

Often we forget everyday courtesies that smooth interactions when we share our living space with another. An important one is the simple greeting. With a greeting we request the attention of the other.

If we don't say, "Hi," or address the other by name before we begin a question or conversation, we invade their privacy in a very real sense. We're demanding their attention instead of requesting it. And we're being disrespectful of whatever activities they are engaged in. If the other frequently responds, "What?" they may be buying the time we have not allowed them to adjust to our presence and to give their attention willingly.

Personal Affirmations

I, (your name), greet others whenever I want their attention.

You, (your name), greet others whenever you want their attention.

(Your name) greets others whenever she/he wants their attention.

We, (your name) and (other's name), greet others whenever we want their attention.

Reciprocal Affirmations

I, (your name), greet you whenever I want your attention.

You, (other's name), greet me whenever you want my attention.

We, (your name) and (other's name), greet each other whenever we want each other's attention.

(Your name) and (other's name) greet each other whenever they want each other's attention.

When someone is upset, how can we help? We may think we know what they did wrong, how they can fix the problem or what's best for them. If we spout the mistakes they made or the obvious or even not-so-obvious ways out of the situation, they will feel worse and have even lower self-esteem. The other isn't really looking to us for solutions. They look to us for empathy. They want to validate their feelings of being upset. This increases their self-esteem.

When another is upset, we need to remember they really want empathy from us, not solutions.

Personal Affirmations

I, (your name), give empathy, not solutions.
You, (your name), give empathy, not solutions.
(Your name) gives empathy, not solutions.
We, (your name) and (other's name), give empathy, not solutions.

Reciprocal Affirmations

I, (your name), give you empathy, not solutions.
You, (other's name), give me empathy, not solutions.
We, (your name) and (other's name), give each other empathy, not solutions.
(Your name) and (other's name) give each other empathy, not solutions.

We may feel we don't want to take the risk of sharing our hopes and dreams with someone else. We may have had dreams long ago that never came true. We may have been stung by broken promises and disappointments. We may fear being criticized as wrong, unrealistic or silly.

But our personal dreams are much more likely to come true if we share them with someone close. When we do this, we take the risk of truly believing in our dreams. We deserve to have unconditional listening and sharing of dreams, and we can ask the other for it.

Personal Affirmations

I, (your name), make opportunities to share my dreams.

You, (your name), make opportunities to share your dreams.

(Your name) makes opportunities to share her/his dreams.

We, (your name) and (other's name), make opportunities to share our dreams.

Reciprocal Affirmations

I, (your name), make opportunities to share my dreams with you.

You, (other's name), make opportunities to share your dreams with me.

We, (your name) and (other's name), make opportunities to share our dreams with each other.

(Your name) and (other's name) make opportunities to share their dreams with each other.

If someone we love is sick or troubled, we help best by sharing our strength. We may be tempted to hurt with them or for them out of sympathy or to tell them how not to hurt out of authority. But each of us must heal ourselves. If we take on another's anger or pain, we share their hurt, not our strength. And we can only really feel the same if we share the same experience.

If we tell them what we would do or would have done, we take control of their lives and interfere with their own decisions for health. Our understanding and appreciation of their feelings — our empathy — will lend them the strength they need.

Personal Affirmations

I, (your name), am empathetic to those in pain.
You, (your name), are empathetic to those in pain.
(Your name) is empathetic to those in pain.
We, (your name) and (other's name), are empathetic to those in pain.

Reciprocal Affirmations

I, (your name), am empathetic to you when you're troubled.
You, (other's name), are empathetic to me when I'm troubled.
We, (your name) and (other's name), are empathetic to each other when we're troubled.
(Your name) and (other's name) are empathetic to each other when they're troubled.

Am I responsible for the success, failure, tone, pain or pleasure of a relationship? Of course I'm partly responsible, but I'm not totally responsible. No matter how much I want a relationship to succeed, I don't control it. I only control half of it.

I do my best to make my relationships work, to make them pleasant and joyful. I realize, however, that my input is only 50 percent of the total. The other person is equally responsible and equally in control. And I can't control the quality of that person's contribution.

Personal Affirmations

I, (your name), am only 50 percent responsible for the success of my relationships.

You, (your name), are only 50 percent responsible for the success of your relationships.

(Your name) is only 50 percent responsible for the success of her/his relationships.

We, (your name) and (other's name), are each only 50 percent responsible for the success of our relationships.

Reciprocal Affirmations

I, (your name), am only 50 percent responsible for the success of our relationship.

You, (other's name), are only 50 percent responsible for the success of our relationship.

We, (your name) and (other's name), are each only 50 percent responsible for the success of our relationship.

(Your name) and (other's name) are each only 50 percent responsible for the success of their relationship.

When we share our visions of the future with our loved ones, we either discover we are incompatible or we allow ourselves to work toward the same or complementary goals that strengthen our relationship.

I enjoy sharing my vision of the future with my loved one. It helps me pin down or articulate some of my goals or desires. Likewise, I enjoy sharing my loved one's vision of the future. It helps me see where they are headed and allows us to form compatible visions.

Personal Affirmations

I, (your name), share my vision of the future with my loved one.

You, (your name), share your vision of the future with your loved one.

(Your name) shares her/his vision of the future with her/his loved one.

We, (your name) and (other's name), share our vision of the future with each other.

Reciprocal Affirmations

I, (your name), share my vision of the future with you.

You, (other's name), share your vision of the future with me.

We, (your name) and (other's name), share our vision of the future with each other.

(Your name) and (other's name) share their vision of the future with each other.

When we choose a companion, we're often attracted to someone different from us. For example, if we're volatile, we may be attracted to someone with a steady mood. Or if we're "old reliable," we may be drawn to someone with exciting flights of enthusiasm.

When we spend lots of time with these people, we may find our temperamental differences cause friction rather than pleasure. But we can cultivate our appreciation of differences. We need to avoid trying to make others like ourselves for our convenience or sense of security. By attending to our own moods, becoming more likable to ourselves and leaving others their own space, we nurture the interest and attraction we first felt.

Personal Affirmations

I, (your name), respect differences of temperament in others.

You, (your name), respect differences of temperament in others.

(Your name) respects differences of temperament in others.

We, (your name) and (other's name), respect differences of temperament in others.

Reciprocal Affirmations

I, (your name), respect your personal temperament.

You, (other's name), respect my personal temperament.

We, (your name) and (other's name), respect differences of temperament in each other.

(Your name) and (other's name) respect differences of temperament in each other.

What makes us want to defend against every little misstatement or accusation about us, even when we know it's said in anger? Sometimes we forget that each of us is in control of our own peace of mind. If we rely on nonstop acceptance and appreciation from others, we give up that control. We try to regain it by setting the other straight, only to find we have escalated a conflict.

Sometimes we think right and truth require us to correct the other's errors or misstatements. But fighting words from another reflect their state of mind and need not affect us. We can maintain our peace of mind by walking away from a fight.

Personal Affirmations

I, (your name), avoid defensiveness when I hear angry words.

You, (your name), avoid defensiveness when you hear angry words.

(Your name) avoids defensiveness when she/he hears angry words.

We, (your name) and (other's name), avoid defensiveness when we hear angry words.

Reciprocal Affirmations

I, (your name), avoid defensiveness when I hear angry words.

You, (other's name), avoid defensiveness when you hear angry words.

We, (your name) and (other's name), avoid defensiveness when we hear angry words.

(Your name) and (other's name) avoid defensiveness when they hear angry words.

Many of us believe anger is a nasty emotion. We may blame it for violent behavior. Or we may think it's inherently offensive and accusatory to others.

But anger, like all other emotions, is neither good nor bad. It's a passing response to changes in our environment. It occurs when things don't go our way. It's okay to feel it. Indeed, we deceive ourselves if we think we don't feel it. What matters is what we do with it.

If I hold onto anger, blame someone else for making me angry or believe I must express it aggressively to let it go, then I, not my anger, am to blame.

Personal Affirmations

I, (your name), let anger come and go without blame.

You, (your name), let anger come and go without blame.

(Your name) lets anger come and go without blame.

We, (your name) and (other's name), let anger come and go without blame.

Reciprocal Affirmations

I, (your name), let anger come and go without blaming you.

You, (other's name), let anger come and go without blaming me.

We, (your name) and (other's name), let anger come and go without blaming each other.

(Your name) and (other's name) let anger come and go without blaming each other.

Each moment we make a choice whether to feel good or bad, positive or negative. No matter what our overall circumstances or the immediate situation, we can exert positive influence on our relationships by becoming more aware of these choices and choosing wisely.

We may have noticed how quickly a child's mood can change with the slightest loving attention from a parent. So we can change with the slightest loving attention to ourselves. And so others can change, too, when we make a choice to give them our loving attention even for a moment. I have the power to improve my own mood and the tone of all my relationships.

Personal Affirmations
I, (your name), project a positive mood.
You, (your name), project a positive mood.
(Your name) projects a positive mood.
We, (your name) and (other's name), project positive moods.

Reciprocal Affirmations
I, (your name), project a positive mood.
You, (other's name), project a positive mood.
We, (your name) and (other's name), project positive moods.
(Your name) and (other's name) project positive moods.

Sometimes we struggle with efforts to forgive others for the hurts and wrongs they have done to us. It may be helpful to learn to forgive ourselves first. If we carry anger or resentment at ourselves for past mistakes, poor judgment, dependency or helplessness, we will find it hard to accept these human traits in others.

Forgiveness is the act of accepting, "giving before," dispensing with judgment. Only if we have judged someone is there any need to forgive. Since we aren't in a position to judge another, judgment is a mistake we've made. We need and deserve to forgive ourselves for it. To open our hearts to others, we must accept our own humanness with self-forgiveness.

Personal Affirmations
I, (your name), forgive myself and others easily.
You, (your name), forgive yourself and others easily.
(Your name) forgives herself/himself and others easily.
We, (your name) and (other's name), forgive ourselves and others easily.

Reciprocal Affirmations
I, (your name), forgive myself and you easily.
You, (other's name), forgive yourself and me easily.
We, (your name) and (other's name), forgive ourselves and each other easily.
(Your name) and (other's name) forgive themselves and each other easily.

One ingredient a successful relationship requires is time — time to be together, time to relate, time to share, time to dream, time to work out problems. The more time we spend together, the closer we get. This happens whether the relationship is with a lover, spouse, child, parent, buddy or co-worker.

If the relationship is important to us, we need to give priority to spending time on it. In this way we assure that we are providing the opportunity for the relationship to grow.

Personal Affirmations

I, (your name), spend time on my important relationships.

You, (your name), spend time on your important relationships.

(Your name) spends time on her/his important relationships.

We, (your name) and (other's name), spend time on our important relationships.

Reciprocal Affirmations

I, (your name), spend time on our relationship.

You, (other's name), spend time on our relationship.

We, (your name) and (other's name), spend time on our relationship.

(Your name) and (other's name) spend time on their relationship.

Conventional wisdom has it that you must adapt yourself to your job and try to keep your personal life from jeopardizing your work. But if the adaptations we're making don't build our self-esteem day by day, we need to change, to discover something we admire in ourselves that can lead us to more meaningful work.

Of course we want to have the option of keeping our present job. But if our work is jeopardizing our personal life, we can look for ways to develop ourselves in directions that will increase our self-esteem. Only if our work is meaningful do we feel whole and able to relate to others well, on or off the job.

Personal Affirmations
I, (your name), deserve meaningful work.
You, (your name), deserve meaningful work.
(Your name) deserves meaningful work.
We, (your name) and (other's name), each deserve meaningful work.

Reciprocal Affirmations
I, (your name), deserve meaningful work.
You, (other's name), deserve meaningful work.
We, (your name) and (other's name), each deserve meaningful work.
(Your name) and (other's name) each deserve meaningful work.

All of us have needs and desires. Even though we may view the needs of those we relate to as important, we must put our own needs and desires first. Basically, we can't love someone else unless we love ourselves. We manifest our self-love by putting ourselves first.

I give priority to my own needs. Only when I've shown my love to myself in this way do I have the love necessary to support others in fulfilling their needs.

Personal Affirmations

It's okay for me, (your name), to love myself.
It's okay for you, (your name), to love yourself.
It's okay for (your name) to love herself/himself.
It's okay for us, (your name) and (other's name), to love ourselves.

Reciprocal Affirmations

It's okay for me, (your name), to love myself.
It's okay for you, (other's name), to love yourself.
It's okay for us, (your name) and (other's name), to love ourselves.
It's okay for (your name) and (other's name) to love themselves.

When we sense a persistent tension in a relationship, we may increase the tension by taking every opportunity to persuade our partner they must change. Perhaps we want them to be more caring, more understanding, a better listener, more interesting, more emotionally independent, slimmer or more open. But our explanations, insistence, urgency or pleading seem only to make things worse. If we are constantly frustrated when our partner denies their need to change, we may also be in denial. We may need to change.

If our behavior isn't leading to solutions, we do need to change. It takes two to create persistent tension, but only one to break it.

Personal Affirmations

I, (your name), am open to changing myself for the better.

You, (your name), are open to changing yourself for the better.

(Your name) is open to changing herself/himself for the better.

We, (your name) and (other's name), are open to changing ourselves for the better.

Reciprocal Affirmations

I, (your name), am open to changing myself for the better.

You, (other's name), are open to changing yourself for the better.

We, (your name) and (other's name), are open to changing ourselves for the better.

(Your name) and (other's name) are open to changing themselves for the better.

If at times we feel a lot of anger, tension and frustration in our relationships, we can help keep the door open to mutual respect and healing communication by attending to the tone of our interactions.

If we show our anger by raising our voice, making threats or speaking profanely, obscenely or crudely, we are projecting our anger outside ourselves. Then it's likely to come back at us. Instead we need to own our anger, admit to ourselves and the other that it's ours and leave room for a common search for a resolution. We can become as sophisticated with our vocabulary of feelings as we have become in our vocabulary of provocative words.

Personal Affirmations

I, (your name), attend to the tone of my interactions.
You, (your name), attend to the tone of your interactions.
(Your name) attends to the tone of her/his interactions.
We, (your name) and (other's name), attend to the tone of our interactions.

Reciprocal Affirmations

I, (your name), attend to the tone of our interactions.
You, (other's name), attend to the tone of our interactions.
We, (your name) and (other's name), attend to the tone of our interactions.
(Your name) and (other's name) attend to the tone of their interactions.

In our modern era we value our rational powers. When we have a result we don't like, we look for causes. We analyze problems to find solutions.

In our relationships, these highly developed skills don't always yield the benefits we expect. In efforts to be rational we may deny someone's right to feelings, including our own. Our effort to find causes can quickly degenerate into placing blame. Attempts to analyze the complexities of a relationship in the heat of a moment can lead to escalated emotion rather than solutions.

In interpersonal crises small or large, we do best to limit our attention to the moment and get a perspective on our own role in it. Then solutions will come.

Personal Affirmations
I, (your name), don't over-rationalize.
You, (your name), don't over-rationalize.
(Your name) doesn't over-rationalize.
We, (your name) and (other's name), don't over-rationalize.

Reciprocal Affirmations
I, (your name), don't over-rationalize.
You, (other's name), don't over-rationalize.
We, (your name) and (other's name), don't over-rationalize.
(Your name) and (other's name) don't over-rationalize.

We all are connected by an energy field that gives us a tendency to resonate with each other. This gives us the power to develop sympathy and empathy. It's also something we can count on in others. In any relationship, the other will tend to reflect the attitude we exhibit.

This means we don't always have to know exactly what to do next, exactly what is right or best, exactly how to fix things. We can have a beneficial influence on another or on our relationship just by being kind and respectful. They will tend then to be more kind and respectful to us, to themselves or to both, and problems will become more manageable.

Personal Affirmations

I, (your name), am kind and respectful to others.

You, (your name), are kind and respectful to others.

(Your name) is kind and respectful to others.

We, (your name) and (other's name), are kind and respectful to others.

Reciprocal Affirmations

I, (your name), am kind and respectful to you.

You, (other's name), are kind and respectful to me.

We, (your name) and (other's name), are kind and respectful to each other.

(Your name) and (other's name) are kind and respectful to each other.

When we have a negative experience, feeling or attitude, we tend to dwell on it. We think about what went wrong, how we could have prevented it and how foolish or stupid we look. How can we get past these feelings and attitudes and get rid of them?

Only one thing gets rid of darkness — light. Likewise, only one thing gets rid of negativity, and that's positive feelings and attitudes. We can only fill our mind with one at a time. The choice is up to us. We can choose the positive.

Personal Affirmations

I, (your name), choose to fill my mind with positive attitudes.

You, (your name), choose to fill your mind with positive attitudes.

(Your name) chooses to fill her/his mind with positive attitudes.

We, (your name) and (other's name), choose to fill our minds with positive attitudes.

Reciprocal Affirmations

I, (your name), choose to fill my mind with positive attitudes.

You, (other's name), choose to fill your mind with positive attitudes.

We, (your name) and (other's name), choose to fill our minds with positive attitudes.

(Your name) and (other's name) choose to fill their minds with positive attitudes.

There is more to love than giving. Receiving is the other half. Many of us receive love in a very negative way. We look for the strings we assume are attached. We immediately deny or devalue ourselves or the expression of love. Or we look for a way to repay each expression of love "tit for tat." This negative outlook gives us a defective receiver.

I need to accept that I am lovable and that I deserve love. When I know this, I can graciously receive love without strings, believing it and realizing there is no "tit for tat."

Personal Affirmations

I, (your name), receive love with no strings attached.
You, (your name), receive love with no strings attached.
(Your name) receives love with no strings attached.
We, (your name) and (other's name), receive love with no strings attached.

Reciprocal Affirmations

I, (your name), receive your love with no strings attached.
You, (other's name), receive my love with no strings attached.
We, (your name) and (other's name), receive each other's love with no strings attached.
(Your name) and (other's name) receive each other's love with no strings attached.

Time is on our side. Sometimes we think we don't have enough time to do what we want, things aren't happening in time or our troubles are lasting too long.

But time becomes an ally if we are patient with ourselves and others. We need to trust our internal timing. Otherwise we fight ourselves, trying to force things that aren't comfortable yet. We are most effective in what we do if we do it when it feels right to us. We must trust others' timing as well. If we think our happiness depends on someone else's timing, we will be tempted to push them, control them and get in the way of a healthy relationship.

Personal Affirmations

I, (your name), trust my internal timing and respect others.'

You, (your name), trust your internal timing and respect others.'

(Your name) trusts her/his internal timing and respects others'.

We, (your name) and (other's name), trust our internal timing and respect others'.

Reciprocal Affirmations

I, (your name), trust my internal timing and respect yours.

You, (other's name), trust your internal timing and respect mine.

We, (your name) and (other's name), trust our own internal timing and respect each other's.

(Your name) and (other's name) trust their own internal timing and respect each other's.

Every relationship presents me with an opportunity to learn. The waiter at the snack shop, the postman, my hair stylist and my significant other all have something to teach me.

By observing others I can learn how they come across or how they accomplish tasks. I can apply those lessons, whether positive or negative, to my own behavior, thus making my behavior more likely to produce my intended result. I will pay attention to others for my own good.

Personal Affirmations

I, (your name), am open to learning from every inter-
    action.

You, (your name), are open to learning from every
    interaction.

(Your name) is open to learning from every interac-
    tion.

We, (your name) and (other's name), are open to
    learning from every interaction.

Reciprocal Affirmations

I, (your name), am open to learning from every inter-
    action.

You, (other's name), are open to learning from every
    interaction.

We, (your name) and (other's name), are open to
    learning from our every interaction.

(Your name) and (other's name) are open to learning
    from their every interaction.

Often we feel ashamed of a mistake we've made. We may think less of ourselves and be too paralyzed to move forward or try again. But everything we do is like riding a bicycle. We can't do it perfectly the first time, but once we have had enough practice, we can do it almost without thinking for the rest of our lives.

Much of our lives is practice in new ways of doing things, behaving toward others and thinking. If we make a mistake, we need only do a little better next time. The only real mistake is to let a mistake of the past detract from our future.

Personal Affirmations

I, (your name), learn new skills through mistakes as well as successes.

You, (your name), learn new skills through mistakes as well as successes.

(Your name) learns new skills through mistakes as well as successes.

We, (your name) and (other's name), learn new skills through mistakes as well as successes.

Reciprocal Affirmations

I, (your name), learn new skills through mistakes as well as successes.

You, (other's name), learn new skills through mistakes as well as successes.

We, (your name) and (other's name), learn new skills through mistakes as well as successes.

(Your name) and (other's name) learn new skills through mistakes as well as successes.

When we share our personal economy with another, financial questions can be a major source of tension — whether overt or covert. To clear the air we need to accept that each is entitled to the money that comes from the giving of their labor or time. The initial choice of what to do with their paycheck must be theirs. We must communicate clearly about shared needs and then trust each other to contribute adequately toward them.

If one of us cannot be trusted, handing over the paycheck without acknowledging rights and choices will not save the relationship. The relationship will end even more surely if trust is lacking than if basic bills aren't paid.

Personal Affirmations

I, (your name), make the choices about how to spend my money.

You, (your name), make the choices about how to spend your money.

(Your name) makes the choices about how to spend her/his money.

We, (your name) and (other's name), each choose how to spend our own money.

Reciprocal Affirmations

I, (your name), make the choices about how to spend my money.

You, (other's name), make the choices about how to spend your money.

We, (your name) and (other's name), each choose how to spend our own money.

(Your name) and (other's name) each choose how to spend their own money.

We all have times when our personal problems seem overwhelming. If we're able to put things back in perspective, the problems don't go away, but they don't seem so big or overwhelming. Instead of ignoring everything but our own problems, we need to look at the rest of the world.

Looking at the national and international news almost any day will help us realize that our problems are rather small on the scale of problems. This can help relieve that overwhelmed feeling. We get the feeling we don't have it so bad after all.

Personal Affirmations
I, (your name), put my problems in perspective.
You, (your name), put your problems in perspective.
(Your name) puts her/his problems in perspective.
We, (your name) and (other's name), put our problems in perspective.

Reciprocal Affirmations
I, (your name), put my problems in perspective.
You, (other's name), put your problems in perspective.
We, (your name) and (other's name), put our problems in perspective.
(Your name) and (other's name) put their problems in perspective.

Other people continually change, as do we. We can't control the change in others, and we shouldn't try to. If the other is close to us, our relationship may be affected by their change. What do we do then?

We must accept their change and its effect on our relationship. Acceptance of others, rather than trying to control or manipulate them, is the key. Then we can communicate our feelings about the changed relationship and make any changes we need to feel comfortable. Of course, our changes may have an additional effect on the relationship.

Personal Affirmations

I, (your name), accept change in others.

You, (your name), accept change in others.

(Your name) accepts change in others.

We, (your name) and (other's name), accept change in others.

Reciprocal Affirmations

I, (your name), accept change in you.

You, (other's name), accept change in me.

We, (your name) and (other's name), accept change in each other.

(Your name) and (other's name) accept change in each other.

When things aren't going our way, we may be tempted to try to force solutions. Our grip on things tightens as we want so much for positive change. But good changes come when we loosen our grip and give other forces a chance to work. We may be in a rut of negativity without knowing it. We need to let good things happen as often as make them happen.

A positive attitude includes patience and hope as much as determination. I need to cultivate the belief that things will change for the better without my assistance. Then I will be primed to recognize the tiny glimmers of change as they come and to encourage them with my enjoyment of them.

Personal Affirmations

I, (your name), am patient and hopeful.
You, (your name), are patient and hopeful.
(Your name) is patient and hopeful.
We, (your name) and (other's name), are patient and hopeful.

Reciprocal Affirmations

I, (your name), am patient and hopeful.
You, (other's name), are patient and hopeful.
We, (your name) and (other's name), are patient and hopeful.
(Your name) and (other's name) are patient and hopeful.

It may be hard to imagine having a positive attitude when things go poorly in our lives and we see things going wrong in the world. Yet the first time we reach out to someone, smile and say something nice — "I like your jacket." — chances are they will smile back and we will feel good. That's the first step to a positive attitude. Try it again a few minutes later. And again. And again. Before long we feel really good and have a positive attitude.

Whenever things seem negative, remember to be nice to someone, even a stranger, and reap the positive rewards. Smiles and good feelings are infectious and soon lead to a positive attitude.

Personal Affirmations
I, (your name), smile my way to a positive attitude.
You, (your name), smile your way to a positive attitude.
(Your name) smiles her/his way to a positive attitude.
We, (your name) and (other's name), smile our way to
   a positive attitude.

Reciprocal Affirmations
I, (your name), smile my way to a positive attitude.
You, (other's name), smile your way to a positive atti-
   tude.
We, (your name) and (other's name), smile our way to
   a positive attitude.
(Your name) and (other's name) smile their way to a
   positive attitude.

Some of us are reluctant to have older friends because they remind us of our own mortality. We don't want to be reminded that we are aging and will be like them. Likewise, many people don't want to be reminded of their age. This fear of a natural process, aging, can also create a sense of urgency in our lives which affects our relationships.

This sense of urgency often upsets our priorities. It may cause us to believe we have to work very hard and earn a lot of money while we're young — but meanwhile we neglect our children or other interests. We can avoid these effects by living fully in the moment.

Personal Affirmations

I, (your name), fully enjoy my current age.
You, (your name), fully enjoy your current age.
(Your name) fully enjoys her/his current age.
We, (your name) and (other's name), fully enjoy our current ages.

Reciprocal Affirmations

I, (your name), fully enjoy my current age.
You, (other's name), fully enjoy your current age.
We, (your name) and (other's name), fully enjoy our current ages.
(Your name) and (other's name) fully enjoy their current ages.

Commitment is something deep within us that we cannot turn on at will. Making a promise of commitment to another alone doesn't ensure faithfulness, no matter how reluctant we are to break promises.

Instead, commitment is a series of choices, a direction of our effort and a plan that must be nurtured. Each day we make a new choice to stay with this direction and to stick with this plan. We need to seek out experiences today that give us the benefits of our commitment. This is the way we nurture it. In a loving relationship joint activities, touching, eye contact, sharing dreams and flirting are all choices we make to nurture our commitment to each other.

Personal Affirmations

I, (your name), choose activities to nurture my commitment.

You, (your name), choose activities to nurture your commitment.

(Your name) chooses activities to nurture her/his commitment.

We, (your name) and (other's name), choose activities to nurture our commitment.

Reciprocal Affirmations

I, (your name), choose activities to nurture my commitment.

You, (other's name), choose activities to nurture your commitment.

We, (your name) and (other's name), choose activities to nurture our commitment.

(Your name) and (other's name) choose activities to nurture their commitment.

When we find someone we admire and want to be with and they return the compliment, we may come to rely on them emotionally to the exclusion of others. For example, if we have cultivated high standards for ourselves and others, and we now find someone who shares them, they seem to bring us together and set us apart from others.

But if we find ourselves constantly sharing criticisms or complaints about others, we will detract from our own humanity and ultimately weaken our bond. If we deny our common bond with all of humanity, we deny a part of ourselves. We can best nurture our close relationships by nurturing all our relationships and believing in people.

Personal Affirmations
I, (your name), believe in people.
You, (your name), believe in people.
(Your name) believes in people.
We, (your name) and (other's name), believe in people.

Reciprocal Affirmations
I, (your name), believe in all people and in you.
You, (other's name), believe in all people and in me.
We, (your name) and (other's name), believe in all
    people and in each other.
(Your name) and (other's name) believe in all people
    and in each other.

What is the appropriate amount of trust in a relationship? It depends on the relationship. You may appropriately take advice from your spouse, while it would be foolish or inappropriate to take advice from a telemarketing stockbroker or someone you just met.

In a close, longstanding relationship, the other cares about your interests. The telemarketing stockbroker is only interested in a commission and has no interest in your investment success. The person you just met falls somewhere in between. The newer and less intimate the relationship, the more like the telemarketing stockbroker and the less like the longstanding spouse.

Personal Affirmations

I, (your name), use my common sense in deciding how much to trust others.

You, (your name), use your common sense in deciding how much to trust others.

(Your name) uses her/his common sense in deciding how much to trust others.

We, (your name) and (other's name), use our common sense in deciding how much to trust others.

Reciprocal Affirmations

I, (your name), use my common sense in deciding how much to trust others.

You, (other's name), use your common sense in deciding how much to trust others.

We, (your name) and (other's name), use our common sense in deciding how much to trust others.

(Your name) and (other's name) use their common sense in deciding how much to trust others.

We are free to divide the chores of daily living any way we want in a relationship. The most important thing is to have both of us agree on the division and remain flexible about reconsidering it if one of us develops different needs or wants.

To achieve agreement and maintain flexibility, we first need to know exactly how we each feel about different chores. I may love to cook but hate to use the dishwasher. Or I may have no objection to filling the dishwasher but may procrastinate when it comes to emptying it. If a chore doesn't get done, we may need to redefine it or break it down. Good communication about daily chores smooths our interactions.

Personal Affirmations

I, (your name), divide chores with confidence and flexibility.

You, (your name), divide chores with confidence and flexibility.

(Your name) divides chores with confidence and flexibility.

We, (your name) and (other's name), divide chores with confidence and flexibility.

Reciprocal Affirmations

I, (your name), divide chores with confidence and flexibility.

You, (other's name), divide chores with confidence and flexibility.

We, (your name) and (other's name), divide chores with confidence and flexibility.

(Your name) and (other's name) divide chores with confidence and flexibility.

We often speak of being angry at something or someone. We yell at someone. We curse or complain about
something. What is our relationship with the other person or thing? Can we control them? Is it our business to
judge them? Do we really know whether they are ultimately right or wrong?

When we find ourselves angry, yelling, cursing or
complaining, let's avoid blaming the other for our state
of mind. Instead, let's take full responsibility for our
emotions and behavior. No person or thing can force us
into any particular state. It's up to us. As we learn to
acknowledge our choice in the matter, we will find it
easier to let go of anger peacefully.

Personal Affirmations
I, (your name), don't blame others for my anger.
You, (your name), don't blame others for your anger.
(Your name) doesn't blame others for her/his anger.
We, (your name) and (other's name), don't blame
    others for our anger.

Reciprocal Affirmations
I, (your name), don't blame you for my anger.
You, (other's name), don't blame me for your anger.
We, (your name) and (other's name), don't blame
    each other for our anger.
(Your name) and (other's name) don't blame each
    other for their anger.

When our lives are filled with job, keeping house, attending to family and planning our future, we can get trapped into noticing only those things over which we think we have some control. We may ignore the larger world, the natural background to our lives.

But the sky, the earth, the rain, the sun, the fleeting clouds and the shifting seasons have long been known to give a fresh perspective to our lives. They inspire us, give us a connection to something greater than ourselves and awaken awe and wonder that restore our youthful enthusiasm. The beauty and tranquility they offer can teach us to find peace in ourselves and with another.

Personal Affirmations

I, (your name), share the wonder of the natural world with another today.

You, (your name), share the wonder of the natural world with another today.

(Your name) shares the wonder of the natural world with another today.

We, (your name) and (other's name), share the wonder of the natural world today.

Reciprocal Affirmations

I, (your name), share the wonder of the natural world with you today.

You, (other's name), share the wonder of the natural world with me today.

We, (your name) and (other's name), share the wonder of the natural world together today.

(Your name) and (other's name) share the wonder of the natural world together today.

Are we impatient with ourselves? Do we expect perfection of ourselves in all things? Are we critical of our mistakes? Do we remember most of the mistakes we ever made? We are human, not perfect.

It's hard to be a good friend to others unless you're a good friend to yourself. Being a good friend means being patient, tolerant or compassionate when things are going poorly, and happy and congratulatory when things are going well. We can be supportive friends for others when we do the same for ourselves.

Personal Affirmations

I, (your name), am my own best friend.

You, (your name), are your own best friend.

(Your name) is her/his own best friend.

We, (your name) and (other's name), are our own
    best friends.

Reciprocal Affirmations

I, (your name), am my own best friend.

You, (other's name), are your own best friend.

We, (your name) and (other's name), are our own
    best friends.

(Your name) and (other's name) are their own best
    friends.

When our attempts to share cheerful news or feelings are met with skepticism, jealousy, impatience or sarcasm, we may be able to change the response by beginning our communication more patiently.

We need to establish rapport with the other. We can do this by noticing the rhythms of their speech and body and adjusting ourselves a bit in that direction. And we can make open-ended, specific inquiries about their lives in a caring way. Most of all, we need to listen actively to their words and respond empathetically. By developing rapport we create an atmosphere of comfort and trust that makes them more able to hear our good news and share our good feelings.

Personal Affirmations

I, (your name), set the stage for my good news.
You, (your name), set the stage for your good news.
(Your name) sets the stage for her/his good news.
We, (your name) and (other's name), set the stage for our good news.

Reciprocal Affirmations

I, (your name), set the stage for my good news.
You, (other's name), set the stage for your good news.
We, (your name) and (other's name), set the stage for our good news.
(Your name) and (other's name) set the stage for their good news.

Our most enjoyable relationships are between equals. It's when we acknowledge each other's equal value and similar humanity that we have room to be ourselves and to grow. But equality gives us challenges that don't exist in a relationship where the line of power goes in only one direction. Decisions that affect the other must be made together in some fashion. And actions must be taken cooperatively.

To make common decisions, we need the spiritual strength to accept that if no decision can be made, the world won't crumble. We need patience and faith. To act cooperatively, we need a healthy understanding of our needs, wants and motivations, as well as flexibility and a willingness to understand others.

Personal Affirmations

I, (your name), cooperate with others as equals.
You, (your name), cooperate with others as equals.
(Your name) cooperates with others as equals.
We, (your name) and (other's name), cooperate with others as equals.

Reciprocal Affirmations

I, (your name), cooperate with you as my equal.
You, (other's name), cooperate with me as your equal.
We, (your name) and (other's name), cooperate with each other as equals.
(Your name) and (other's name) cooperate with each other as equals.

Sometimes we wonder if there is a middle ground between optimism and pessimism. In our effort to control our future, we may project, predict, look for something better or fear for something worse. The path out of this ping-pong thinking is temporal — where are we focusing our attention in the spectrum of time?

Bliss is ours if we focus our attention on the present. We can be wholly in touch only with the present. We can know reality only in the present. If right now we are alive and thinking any of these thoughts, we have reason for joy. If we have one person today with whom to share a thought, we can revel in a moment of bliss.

Personal Affirmations

I, (your name), revel in my moments of bliss.

You, (your name), revel in your moments of bliss.

(Your name) revels in her/his moments of bliss.

We, (your name) and (other's name), revel in our moments of bliss.

Reciprocal Affirmations

I, (your name), revel in our moments of bliss.

You, (other's name), revel in our moments of bliss.

We, (your name) and (other's name), revel in our moments of bliss.

(Your name) and (other's name) revel in their moments of bliss.

Has someone close to us complained about our weight, cooking, drinking, housecleaning, the way we load the toilet paper or the way we squeeze the toothpaste? Do we try to change our behavior, feel guilty or apologize, only to find they haven't let up but just changed what they complain about?

If we can't please another no matter what we do, we may need to accept that many complainers are just complainers. They will always find something to complain about. Our efforts to please them or remove the offending behavior will be to no avail, because we aren't perfect and they will always find some other behavior to complain about. We need only please ourselves.

Personal Affirmations

I, (your name), don't try to please complainers.
You, (your name), don't try to please complainers.
(Your name) doesn't try to please complainers.
We, (your name) and (other's name), don't try to please complainers.

Reciprocal Affirmations

I, (your name), don't try to please complainers.
You, (other's name), don't try to please complainers.
We, (your name) and (other's name), don't try to please complainers.
(Your name) and (other's name) don't try to please complainers.

At times we feel we don't see enough of our loved ones. We get jealous of their job, friends, activities or even children. We fear one or all of these things will become more important to them than we are and cause us to lose them.

Jealousy arises out of our fear of loss. We often react to the fear in a negative way, trying to control the other. We need to trust that the other is doing what's best for them. A relationship built on bondage isn't love. One built on freedom is. We need to forget about jealousy and give others the freedom to love us.

Personal Affirmations

I, (your name), give others the freedom to love me.
You, (your name), give others the freedom to love you.
(Your name) gives others the freedom to love her/him.
We, (your name) and (other's name), give others the freedom to love us.

Reciprocal Affirmations

I, (your name), give you the freedom to love me.
You, (other's name), give me the freedom to love you.
We, (your name) and (other's name), give the other the freedom to love us.
(Your name) and (other's name) give the other the freedom to love them.

What can I do when another's behavior bothers me? For instance, if the other is depressed and I don't want to deal with that now, what can I do? I can't change their behavior and I mustn't tell them what to do.

I can, of course, remove myself from the situation. I can also model behavior that I feel good about. I can be cheerful and go about my business. Sometimes a good example rubs off. In any case, modeling healthy behavior while being understanding is the most I can do to help someone else.

Personal Affirmations
I, (your name), set a good example.
You, (your name), set a good example.
(Your name) sets a good example.
We, (your name) and (other's name), set good examples.

Reciprocal Affirmations
I, (your name), set a good example.
You, (other's name), set a good example.
We, (your name) and (other's name), set good examples.
(Your name) and (other's name) set good examples.

Sharing good news or happy emotions really feels good! That's the part of life and relationships we all look foward to. It's the fun part.

Both the person who shares and the other can enjoy the good news of happy emotions. The other isn't only happy for the person sharing. The good feelings are infectious. They bring pleasure to both and enrich the relationship. We enjoy life together, which was probably our goal when we started our relationshp in the first place.

Personal Affirmations

I, (your name), share happy emotions with others.

You, (your name), share happy emotions with others.

(Your name) shares happy emotions with others.

We, (your name) and (other's name), share happy emotions with others.

Reciprocal Affirmations

I, (your name), share happy emotions with you.

You, (other's name), share happy emotions with me.

We, (your name) and (other's name), share happy emotions with each other.

(Your name) and (other's name) share happy emotions with each other.

Taking stock periodically can give us a wonderful feeling. It's a time of reviewing and appreciating all of our accomplishments, changes and progress over a past period. The period can be annual on our birthday, New Year's Day or some other significant or easy-to-remember date. It can be quarterly at the start of the seasons, or even monthly.

Realizing how much we've grown over the past period gives confidence, strength and inspiration for the future. After we've taken stock of ourselves, we can take stock of our relationship, either on our own or together.

Personal Affirmations

I, (your name), take stock of myself periodically.
You, (your name), take stock of yourself periodically.
(Your name) takes stock of herself/himself periodically.
We, (your name) and (other's name), take stock of ourselves periodically.

Reciprocal Affirmations

I, (your name), take stock of myself periodically.
You, (other's name), take stock of yourself periodically.
We, (your name) and (other's name), take stock of our relationship periodically.
(Your name) and (other's name) take stock of their relationship periodically.

When we share our thoughts and feelings with another, we seek to build intimacy and mutual understanding. These will be jeopardized if we press the other to reveal more than they are comfortable with. I have no right to know more about another than they are willing to share. Nor does another have the right to have me share more than I want to.

When we try to accept people as they are, this doesn't mean we must know them totally before we decide whether we can accept them. It means we accept them with any closed doors they choose to keep. By the same token, we can maintain our privacy at any level we choose.

Personal Affirmations

I, (your name), maintain my privacy and respect that of others.

You, (your name), maintain your privacy and respect that of others.

(Your name) maintains her/his privacy and respects that of others.

We, (your name) and (other's name), each maintain our privacy and respect that of others.

Reciprocal Affirmations

I, (your name), maintain my privacy and respect yours.

You, (other's name), maintain your privacy and respect mine.

We, (your name) and (other's name), each maintain our privacy and respect each other's.

(Your name) and (other's name) each maintain our privacy and respect each other's.

Sometimes I have high expectations for others. If I communicate my expectations either outright or subtly through my attitude or reactions, I can harm the other's self-esteem.

If the other tries and fails to meet my expectations, it can lead to a devastating feeling of failure. Yet meeting my expectations can also lead to a lack of self-esteem. Carrying out someone else's agenda rather than our own injures self-esteem because it teaches us we aren't important. I will expect others to do only what they choose for themselves.

Personal Affirmations

I, (your name), let others make their own choices.
You, (your name), let others make their own choices.
(Your name) lets others make their own choices.
We, (your name) and (other's name), let others make their own choices.

Reciprocal Affirmations

I, (your name), let you make your own choices.
You, (other's name), let me make my own choices.
We, (your name) and (other's name), each let the other make their own choices.
(Your name) and (other's name) each let the other make their own choices.

Are there ways to cultivate the lighter side of life? Can we increase our chances to have a little chuckle, to release tension with a laugh? We may take ourselves too seriously or be constantly concerned with what others think of us. We may seek to prove how rational, reasonable, intelligent, quick or smart we are. We may premeditate every move because someone near might get the impression we are foolish, stupid, silly, uneducated or uninformed.

Our lives will hold more joy and meaning if we accept that there is always someone who might call us foolish. We need to follow our intuitions and trust those we care about to laugh with us rather than at us.

Personal Affirmations

I, (your name), cultivate lighter moments without feeling foolish.

You, (your name), cultivate lighter moments without feeling foolish.

(Your name) cultivates lighter moments without feeling foolish.

We, (your name) and (other's name), cultivate lighter moments without feeling foolish.

Reciprocal Affirmations

I, (your name), cultivate lighter moments without feeling foolish.

You, (other's name), cultivate lighter moments without feeling foolish.

We, (your name) and (other's name), cultivate lighter moments without feeling foolish.

(Your name) and (other's name) cultivate lighter moments without feeling foolish.

When we're emotionally down, depressed or discouraged, we need others. Others, especially those close to us, can help cheer us, providing we give them a chance instead of taking it all out on them.

Others can let us know we're not alone through empathy. They can help us see humor when nothing seems funny. Through their love they show us what's really important in life. We need only give them a chance. We need to remember it's a sign of strength to know when we need help.

And we can do the same for them when the situation is reversed.

Personal Affirmations

I, (your name), let others help me when I'm down.

You, (your name), let others help you when you're down.

(Your name) lets others help her/him when she's/he's down.

We, (your name) and (other's name), let others help us when we're down.

Reciprocal Affirmations

I, (your name), let you help me when I'm down.

You, (other's name), let me help you when you're down.

We, (your name) and (other's name), let the other help us when we're down.

(Your name) and (other's name) let the other help them when they're down.

Each of us has a preferred way of experiencing our dreams for the future. Some see a vision such as a cliffside home or an adoring audience. Some feel themselves getting a promotion or crying at a wedding. Others can hear people's praise or the sounds of a tropical surf.

Sharing these dreams with our loved one helps us grow in the same direction. In our leisure time, on vacation or a Saturday night out, we can talk about our dreams and be specific about our preferred sensory perceptions. We can listen with a nonjudgmental, open attitude to the other's dreams and explore together the details of how the dreams might mesh.

Personal Affirmations

I, (your name), build common dreams with my loved one.

You, (your name), build common dreams with your loved one.

(Your name) builds common dreams with her/his loved one.

We, (your name) and (other's name), build common dreams together.

Reciprocal Affirmations

I, (your name), build common dreams with you.

You, (other's name), build common dreams with me.

We, (your name) and (other's name), build common dreams together.

(Your name) and (other's name) build common dreams together.

It's true that opposites attract. We're often drawn to people who epitomize unexplored parts of ourselves. If we're steady and reliable, we may be attracted to someone changeable and spontaneous. If we're aggressive and gregarious, we may be attracted to someone shy and quiet.

In a long-standing relationship these differences that brought us together may begin to grate on us. We may crave someone close who's "just like us." But complementing each other works beautifully if we avoid judging the other's moods and processes and instead accept, respect and enjoy our different creative energies. It helps us to widen and balance our emotional experience of life.

Personal Affirmations

I, (your name), respect others' moods and processes.
You, (your name), respect others' moods and processes.
(Your name) respects others' moods and processes.
We, (your name) and (other's name), respect others'
    moods and processes.

Reciprocal Affirmations

I, (your name), respect your moods and processes.
You, (other's name), respect my moods and processes.
We, (your name) and (other's name), respect each
    other's moods and processes.
(Your name) and (other's name) respect each other's
    moods and processes.

If we put all our eggs in one basket, we risk being lopsided. If we focus all our expectations of love, support and perfection into our romantic relationship, we cut ourselves off from the joys of a broader base of human contact. And we lay a burden on our partner that grows heavier with time.

We can learn to cultivate new friendships outside our primary relationship or look up old friends from the past. An important first step is to select someone we feel comfortable with and then learn to be a good listener. As we build their trust this way, we learn to trust them. We feel ourselves opening up to richer friendships.

Personal Affirmations
I, (your name), am attracting friends by careful listening.
You, (your name), are attracting friends by careful listening.
(Your name) is attracting friends by careful listening.
We, (your name) and (other's name), are attracting friends by careful listening.

Reciprocal Affirmations
I, (your name), am attracting friends by careful listening.
You, (other's name), are attracting friends by careful listening.
We, (your name) and (other's name), are attracting friends by careful listening.
(Your name) and (other's name) are attracting friends by careful listening.

In our goal-oriented society, we often choose goals or benchmarks for even our most intimate encounters. We may feel we have failed without an orgasm or some particular kind of orgasm, for example. But if we are working toward a goal in each sexual encounter, we may sacrifice spontaneous enjoyment and put a wall between us and our partner.

We may need to reconsider our goals for intimacy. When we are driving a car, we need our designated goal to give us a direction. In sex, our deepest natural impulse gives us the needed direction. The only goal we need is one for the present moment, such as fully enjoying ourselves, our partner or our union.

Personal Affirmations

I, (your name), focus my goals for intimacy on the moment.

You, (your name), focus your goals for intimacy on the moment.

(Your name) focuses her/his goals for intimacy on the moment.

We, (your name) and (other's name), focus our goals for intimacy on the moment.

Reciprocal Affirmations

I, (your name), focus my goals for intimacy on the moment.

You, (other's name), focus your goals for intimacy on the moment.

We, (your name) and (other's name), focus our goals for intimacy on the moment.

(Your name) and (other's name) focus their goals for intimacy on the moment.

How we behave has a big effect on how we feel. If we're feeling down, but make ourselves smile at the next person we see or laugh at the next silly situation we see, it's hard to stay glum. We've all experienced this, and now modern science has discovered why. When we smile, laugh or do other happy things, our brain releases endorphins which cause us to experience pleasure.

We can program ourselves to have good experiences when we interact with others. Behaving in a positive happy way when we interact helps us enjoy our relationships.

Personal Affirmations

I, (your name), use my behavior to improve my mood.

You, (your name), use your behavior to improve your mood.

(Your name) uses her/his behavior to improve her/his mood.

We, (your name) and (other's name), use our behavior to improve our moods.

Reciprocal Affirmations

I, (your name), use my behavior to improve my mood.

You, (other's name), use your behavior to improve your mood.

We, (your name) and (other's name), use our behavior to improve our moods.

(Your name) and (other's name) use their behavior to improve their moods.

Anger is the emotion we feel when people don't behave the way we expect. At its core is an emotional investment we've made in something beyond our control. We can't control another person. We can avoid a lot of anger by investing emotional energy only in things we can control, namely ourselves, our attitudes and the tone and contributions we make to our relationships.

If we do feel anger, we need to notice what expectations we have mistakenly had for others that set us up for anger. Then we need to acknowledge the emotion to ourselves and to another and let it go.

Personal Affirmations

I, (your name), release others from my expectations.

You, (your name), release others from your expectations.

(Your name) releases others from her/his expectations.

We, (your name) and (other's name), release others from our expectations.

Reciprocal Affirmations

I, (your name), release you from my expectations.

You, (other's name), release me from your expectations.

We, (your name) and (other's name), release each other from our expectations.

(Your name) and (other's name) release each other from their expectations.

If misery loves company, the opposite is also true. Joy attracts joy. The essential connection between us all allows a resonance between us. Good vibrations projected from me stimulate good vibrations in those around me.

Like a tuning fork imbued with life, I can strike my own tone each day. I can choose to feel happy today with no change at all in my outside circumstances. I can start a reverberation of comfort and joy that will affect the people and things around me and how I perceive them.

However small these effects, they will grow as I hold my tone. And they will grow faster than I think.

Personal Affirmations

I, (your name), set a happy tone for myself.
You, (your name), set a happy tone for yourself.
(Your name) sets a happy tone for herself/himself.
We, (your name) and (other's name), set a happy tone
    for ourselves.

Reciprocal Affirmations

I, (your name), set a happy tone for myself.
You, (other's name), set a happy tone for yourself.
We, (your name) and (other's name), set a happy tone
    for ourselves.
(Your name) and (other's name) set a happy tone for
    themselves.

In order to be truly kind to others and to inspire others to treat us kindly, we must first be kind to ourselves. If we're being impatient, demanding, resentful or angry with ourselves, we will be unable to sustain a healthy attitude toward others. And others tend to treat us as we treat ourselves. We teach others how to treat us.

Each of us does the best we can. We are entitled to be patient, gentle and understanding with ourselves. We need to be compassionate and respectful toward ourselves. And we need to celebrate our innate drive to seek a better life with those around us. We need to be our own best friend.

Personal Affirmations

I, (your name), am kind and compassionate with myself.

You, (your name), are kind and compassionate with yourself.

(Your name) is kind and compassionate with herself/himself.

We, (your name) and (other's name), are kind and compassionate with ourselves.

Reciprocal Affirmations

I, (your name), am kind and compassionate with myself.

You, (other's name), are kind and compassionate with yourself.

We, (your name) and (other's name), are kind and compassionate with ourselves.

(Your name) and (other's name) are kind and compassionate with themselves.

Sometimes we think we need a new relationship to solve our problems. Yet our long-term relationships have special value. They give a special intimacy and understanding that comes from repeated interaction over a long period. We feel a sense of stability from them that we don't get from our newer relationships.

I need to keep my long-term relationships fresh to prevent staleness. I realize that a long-term relationship isn't static because it's old. As in everything else, the only constant is change. I willingly expend the time and energy necessary to nurture my long-term relationships.

Personal Affirmations

I, (your name), nurture my long-term relationships.

You, (your name), nurture your long-term relationships.

(Your name) nurtures her/his long-term relationships.

We, (your name) and (other's name), nurture our long-term relationships.

Reciprocal Affirmations

I, (your name), nurture our long-term relationship.

You, (other's name), nurture our long-term relationship.

We, (your name) and (other's name), nurture our long-term relationship.

(Your name) and (other's name) nurture their long-term relationship.

Often we worry about how we're going to share our negative feelings with another, but we don't spend any time on framing our words when we have positive things to impart. No matter how difficult or negative our day, if we have one good feeling and know what to do with it, we can change the whole tone of our day.

A little gratitude, humor, good cheer, smile or contented sigh given to another in a thoughtful manner not only brightens their day but brightens our own. Focusing on small positives isn't an illusory escape from our troubles; it's a realistic tool for beginning change from within.

Personal Affirmations
I, (your name), nurture little positives in my life.
You, (your name), nurture little positives in your life.
(Your name) nurtures little positives in her/his life.
We, (your name) and (other's name), nurture little positives in our lives.

Reciprocal Affirmations
I, (your name), nurture little positives in our lives.
You, (other's name), nurture little positives in our lives.
We, (your name) and (other's name), nurture little positives in our lives.
(Your name) and (other's name) nurture little positives in their lives.

One of the ways we build relationships is through doing things together. It's an opportunity to share common interests, explore the other's interests or just spend time together. We share the fun and gain understanding of what the other likes or doesn't like and why. We may also talk about many other things just because we are together and have the opportunity.

It's rare to have and difficult to maintain a relationship without common experiences. They are the key to our continuing interest. They are the basis of marriage, love, co-worker and parent-child relationships.

Because I value my current relationships, I will create opportunities to do things together.

Personal Affirmations

I, (your name), spend time doing things with others.
You, (your name), spend time doing things with others.
(Your name) spends time doing things with others.
We, (your name) and (other's name), spend time doing things with others.

Reciprocal Affirmations

I, (your name), spend time doing things with you.
You, (other's name), spend time doing things with me.
We, (your name) and (other's name), spend time doing things together.
(Your name) and (other's name) spend time doing things together.

In a new relationship we find it exciting to discover common feelings from our separate experiences. Two people from different backgrounds find how much they share. It validates us and makes us feel more alive.

As the relationship deepens, separate interests and activities can have the opposite effect. We feel threatened by the other not being just like us or having connections that don't involve us.

But sharing by separate and equal people is what keeps a relationship strong. Neither should dominate the other, nor should we become the same. Instead we can continue to share our excitement over our different friends, interests, hobbies, work and perspectives.

Personal Affirmations

I, (your name), have separate connections that enrich my relationships.

You, (your name), have separate connections that enrich your relationships.

(Your name) has separate connections that enrich her/his relationships.

We, (your name) and (other's name), have separate connections that enrich our relationships.

Reciprocal Affirmations

I, (your name), have separate connections that enrich our relationship.

You, (other's name), have separate connections that enrich our relationship.

We, (your name) and (other's name), have separate connections that enrich our relationship.

(Your name) and (other's name) have separate connections that enrich their relationship.

Does the health of someone close to you concern you? Do you know what they should do for better health or longevity? Do you want them to stop smoking, lose weight, eat better or stop drinking? We justify our desire and even actions to control others by saying we don't want to lose them, it will make our lives more pleasant or it proves we care.

We need to work on ourselves and our own problems and let others work on their own. Others don't want to hear their problems from us, even if we're right, just as we don't want to hear what they have to say about any bad habits or poor choices of ours. We may suggest options from time to time, but repetition and nagging will backfire.

Personal Affirmations
I, (your name), don't take on reforming others.
You, (your name), don't take on reforming others.
(Your name) doesn't take on reforming others.
*We, (your name) and (other's name), don't take on
    reforming others.*

Reciprocal Affirmations
I, (your name), don't take on reforming you.
You, (other's name), don't take on reforming me.
*We, (your name) and (other's name), don't take on
    reforming each other.*
*(Your name) and (other's name) don't take on re-
    forming each other.*

Anger is a natural emotion that helps us let go of tension from not getting what we want. So often we hear, "You shouldn't be angry." Or, "Anger leads to no good." Or, "So you're angry, what are you going to do about it?"

We try to avoid angry outbursts, angry words. But anger isn't wrong or dangerous. It doesn't have to lead to anything, nor must we do anything about it. Trouble comes when we bottle it up or act it out thoughtlessly.

Anger isn't "at" anybody. We own the feeling and don't need an object. If we express our feeling simply by saying, "I feel angry," to someone who can understand, we feel calmed with no ill effects.

Personal Affirmations

I, (your name), accept angry feelings without shame or blame.

You, (your name), accept angry feelings without shame or blame.

(Your name) accepts angry feelings without shame or blame.

We, (your name) and (other's name), accept angry feelings without shame or blame.

Reciprocal Affirmations

I, (your name), accept angry feelings without shame or blame.

You, (other's name), accept angry feelings without shame or blame.

We, (your name) and (other's name), accept angry feelings without shame or blame.

(Your name) and (other's name) accept angry feelings without shame or blame.

Sexual relationships work on the same principles as other relationships. We enrich our sex lives by strengthening our sexual relationship.

The more commitment, communication and mutual support, the stronger the relationship. Commitment implies attention to what is actually happening — our present mutual enjoyment of each other — rather than an imaginary act with some movie star. Communicating our needs and desires to our sex partner helps us satisfy and enjoy each other. Mutual support in the sexual arena means helping when there are difficulties or seeing that both are fully satisfied. Focusing on my sexual relationship makes it more rewarding.

Personal Affirmations

I, (your name), work on building my sexual relationship.

You, (your name), work on building your sexual relationship.

(Your name) works on building her/his sexual relationship.

We, (your name) and (other's name), work on building our sexual relationship.

Reciprocal Affirmations

I, (your name), work on building our sexual relationship.

You, (other's name), work on building our sexual relationship.

We, (your name) and (other's name), work on building our sexual relationship.

(Your name) and (other's name) work on building their sexual relationship.

In a media-drenched age, we are quickly labeled as part of an identifiable generation, often as short as five years or so — the Vietnam generation, the hippies, the flower children, the yuppies or the "me" generation. In school, job and neighborhood, we seem to be thrown together almost entirely with people our own age.

It can be enjoyable to cultivate relationships with people of different generations, whether there are five, 25 or 55 years between us. Younger people keep our perceptions fresh while they help us appreciate all we have learned. Older people pull us out of the immediate stress of today while they help us appreciate the continuity of life.

Personal Affirmations
I, (your name), get along with people of all ages.
You, (your name), get along with people of all ages.
(Your name) gets along with people of all ages.
We, (your name) and (other's name), get along with people of all ages.

Reciprocal Affirmations
I, (your name), get along with people of all ages.
You, (other's name), get along with people of all ages.
We, (your name) and (other's name), get along with people of all ages.
(Your name) and (other's name) get along with people of all ages.

We must beware of generosity that is really a form of self-denial in order to get attention. As children we may have picked up the idea that sacrificing our needs and wants was generosity. But all great altruists say they give because it feels so good for them. They give out of abundance, not scarcity or sacrifice.

In our relationships we need to give what we feel abundant in, not our last dime or our most precious hour of the day. Reinforcing a perception of limited time, money or resources makes us feel less generous instead of more. Let us begin by being generous just with our love.

Personal Affirmations
I, (your name), am generous with my love.
You, (your name), are generous with your love.
(Your name) is generous with her/his love.
We, (your name) and (other's name), are generous with our love.

Reciprocal Affirmations
I, (your name), give my love to you generously.
You, (other's name), give your love to me generously.
We, (your name) and (other's name), give our love to each other generously.
(Your name) and (other's name) give their love to each other generously.

Sometimes we're so busy in our daily lives that we feel as if the other person in a relationship is a stranger. We may pass them in the bedroom or the kitchen, but we're both so intent and hurried that we don't really interact. At the end of the day, we don't feel close to each other.

Taking a moment whenever we pass for a loving word, a hug or a smile, can connect us with the other and allow us to feel close instead of like strangers. The few seconds it takes to hug, smile or speak won't set us back in our hurried life. It will improve our outlook on life and our relationship.

Personal Affirmations

I, (your name), take a moment for a hug, smile or loving word.

You, (your name), take a moment for a hug, smile or loving word.

(Your name) takes a moment for a hug, smile or loving word.

We, (your name) and (other's name), take a moment for a hug, smile or loving word.

Reciprocal Affirmations

I, (your name), take a moment to give you a hug, smile or loving word.

You, (other's name), take a moment to give me a hug, smile or loving word.

We, (your name) and (other's name), take a moment to give each other a hug, smile or loving word.

(Your name) and (other's name) take a moment to give each other a hug, smile or loving word.

Immediate gratification is available everywhere today. Fast food, cheap video and more dangerous and destructive pastimes are all readily available to almost anyone. We can get confused between these immediate gratifications and enjoyment of life. When our relationships aren't meeting our expectations, we may seek enjoyment by escaping into these immediate gratifications. Or we may reject enjoyment itself by associating it in our mind with gratifications that we have virtuously rejected.

Just because we reject much of what has been called "fun" in our current society, we aren't ineligible for enjoyment. Real enjoyment of life comes from within. We deserve it and can have it every day of our lives, even if our relationships are less than ideal.

Personal Affirmations
I, (your name), deserve to really enjoy my daily life.
You, (your name), deserve to really enjoy your daily life.
(Your name) deserves to really enjoy her/his daily life.
We, (your name) and (other's name), deserve to really enjoy our daily life.

Reciprocal Affirmations
I, (your name), deserve to really enjoy my daily life.
You, (other's name), deserve to really enjoy your daily life.
We, (your name) and (other's name), deserve to really enjoy our daily life.
(Your name) and (other's name) deserve to really enjoy their daily life.

Courtesy is an interpersonal tool that smooths our passings through the same space with another. To be courteous to others, we must have esteem for ourselves. We must believe we matter, that we are important enough to announce our arrivals and say good-bye when we depart.

Sometimes we sneak into a room, hoping no one will notice or thinking we will avoid disturbing anyone. We may be trying to avoid friction or the hassle of an interruption in our affairs or theirs. But we are short-changing ourselves and building tension by not recognizing the intrinsic importance of each of us. A simple greeting or farewell will acknowledge our sharing of the same space.

Personal Affirmations

I, (your name), acknowledge my own value by greeting others.

You, (your name), acknowledge your own value by greeting others.

(Your name) acknowledges her/his own value by greeting others.

We, (your name) and (other's name), acknowledge our own value by greeting others.

Reciprocal Affirmations

I, (your name), acknowledge my own value by greeting you.

You, (other's name), acknowledge your own value by greeting me.

We, (your name) and (other's name), acknowledge our own value by greeting each other.

(Your name) and (other's name) acknowledge their own value by greeting each other.

Do we dwell on one or more of our unattractive qualities? Does the resulting depression cause us to stuff ourselves with junk food or indulge some other bad habit and feel even more unattractive? At this point our self-esteem is on the low end of the scale.

Although everyone has some unattractive qualities, it helps to focus on our good points. We each have a number of attractive qualities. If we emphasize the good points, we will have high self-esteem and realize we are attractive to others. Remember, there's somebody for everybody, somebody who appreciates your good qualities.

Personal Affirmations
I, (your name), focus on my good points.
You, (your name), focus on your good points.
(Your name) focuses on her/his good points.
We, (your name) and (other's name), focus on our good points.

Reciprocal Affirmations
I, (your name), focus on my good points.
You, (other's name), focus on your good points.
We, (your name) and (other's name), focus on our good points.
(Your name) and (other's name) focus on each other's good points.

With patience we can influence others. Telling or
forcing them to change won't do it. Accepting them and
listening to them, exactly where they are, will. We acknowledge their right to be as they are and we give
them the space to change as they see fit. At the same
time, we connect with them on the energy level. We
tend to resonate together as long as we have that connection. We establish rapport so they are more able to
accept the greater calm, more relaxed mood and greater
kindness and clarity that we are cultivating.

If we rely on our human connection and not on force,
we will have a happier influence on others.

Personal Affirmations

I, (your name), patiently establish rapport with others.
You, (your name), patiently establish rapport with others.
(Your name) patiently establishes rapport with others.
We, (your name) and (other's name), patiently estab-
*   lish rapport with others.*

Reciprocal Affirmations

I, (your name), patiently establish rapport with you.
You, (other's name), patiently establish rapport with me.
We, (your name) and (other's name), patiently estab-
*   lish rapport with each other.*
(Your name) and (other's name) patiently establish
*   rapport with each other.*

What tools do we want used on us in our relationship? Do we want to be controlled, manipulated or pulled against our will? Or would we respond better to loving trust, caring and kindness?

When we give what we would like to receive — caring, kindness and trust — we open ourselves to receiving. It's almost impossible to receive trust, kindness and caring if we have a manipulating, grabbing, controlling attitude. In the words of the Golden Rule, "Do unto others as you would have them do unto you."

Personal Affirmations

I, (your name), give kindness, caring and trust to others.

You, (your name), give kindness, caring and trust to others.

(Your name) gives kindness, caring and trust to others.

We, (your name) and (other's name), give kindness, caring and trust to others.

Reciprocal Affirmations

I, (your name), give kindness, caring and trust to you.

You, (other's name), give kindness, caring and trust to me.

We, (your name) and (other's name), give each other kindness, caring and trust.

(Your name) and (other's name) give each other kindness, caring and trust.

Anger can lead to a fight when others try to pin the blame for their anger on us. Others seem to assume that we cause their anger and they have no choice in their response. They may feel righteous about it, speaking and acting as if they have a monopoly on the truth. It's no surprise when we become defensive and a fight begins.

But we can defuse their anger by carefully listening and by acknowledging their choice to be angry without taking on blame. When I feel defensive, I can quietly acknowledge anger by saying, "I hear you. You feel angry because of what I did." An angry person mostly wants just to be heard.

Personal Affirmations

I, (your name), hear another's anger without taking on blame.

You, (your name), hear another's anger without taking on blame.

(Your name) hears another's anger without taking on blame.

We, (your name) and (other's name), hear another's anger without taking on blame.

Reciprocal Affirmations

I, (your name), hear your anger without taking on blame.

You, (other's name), hear my anger without taking on blame.

We, (your name) and (other's name), hear each other's anger without taking on blame.

(Your name) and (other's name) hear each other's anger without taking on blame.

Most of us love to give advice. We think we can see clearly where others went wrong and what they should do. We offer advice with pure motives — we want to help the others because we love them. When they don't take our advice and their problems continue, we get frustrated and may criticize, complain or accuse.

What's wrong here? First, we have no control over another's actions. We shouldn't get so involved that we feel frustrated if they don't do what we suggested. Second, advice is rarely what others want. When a person follows advice, they get the message that they can't solve their own problems, thus lowering their self-esteem. They really want good listening, affirmation and validation, not advice.

Personal Affirmations

I, (your name), offer advice without investing my ego.

You, (your name), offer advice without investing your ego.

(Your name) offers advice without investing her/his ego.

We, (your name) and (other's name), offer advice without investing our egos.

Reciprocal Affirmations

I, (your name), offer you advice without investing my ego.

You, (other's name), offer me advice without investing your ego.

We, (your name) and (other's name), offer each other advice without investing our egos.

(Your name) and (other's name) offer each other advice without investing their egos.

The most powerful thing we can do to affirm another in our interactions is to look into their eyes. Eye contact acknowledges and lets them know that they have our full attention. If we look at their hands, at our hands, at their lips, into the distance, out the window or up at the ceiling, we aren't making the direct connection that eye contact can give us.

If we chronically feel unappreciated in our conversations with someone close, we can improve things by directing our eyes to theirs. The simplest way to have them do the same is to say their name often in a loving way during our conversation.

Personal Affirmations
I, (your name), connect with others eye-to-eye.
You, (your name), connect with others eye-to-eye.
(Your name) connects with others eye-to-eye.
We, (your name) and (other's name), connect with others eye-to-eye.

Reciprocal Affirmations
I, (your name), connect with you eye-to-eye.
You, (other's name), connect with me eye-to-eye.
We, (your name) and (other's name), connect with each other eye-to-eye.
(Your name) and (other's name) connect with each other eye-to-eye.

Relationships are meant to be enjoyed. We would have given them up long ago if they weren't. Each day we must find ways to enjoy each other. We can appreciate why we were drawn to the other, focus on what we like about them, enjoy their good motives, remember good times or enjoy a characteristic expression, stance, gesture or turn of phrase.

If problems arise, it can be helpful to just pull back a little, breathe deeply, let up, let go and decide to enjoy the other.

Personal Affirmations
I, (your name), enjoy my relationships.
You, (your name), enjoy your relationships.
(Your name) enjoys her/his relationships.
We, (your name) and (other's name), enjoy our relationships.

Reciprocal Affirmations
I, (your name), enjoy you.
You, (other's name), enjoy me.
We, (your name) and (other's name), enjoy our relationship.
(Your name) and (other's name) enjoy their relationship.

Difficult problems — money, romance, job or family relationships — produce anxieties. We don't know what to do, there seems to be no acceptable solution and we panic. That's anxiety. Perhaps our stomach knots up or we get a headache or some other physical manifestation.

We need time — perhaps a little time to think and consider the options, perhaps more time to sort out things until an acceptable solution becomes clear. We need to accept that the solution to the problem will come with the passage of time. The cure for anxiety is attention to something else as we await the passage of time.

Personal Affirmations

I, (your name), cure my anxieties with time and patience.

You, (your name), cure your anxieties with time and patience.

(Your name) cures her/his anxieties with time and patience.

We, (your name) and (other's name), cure our anxieties with time and patience.

Reciprocal Affirmations

I, (your name), cure my anxieties with time and patience.

You, (other's name), cure your anxieties with time and patience.

We, (your name) and (other's name), cure our anxieties with time and patience.

(Your name) and (other's name) cure their anxieties with time and patience.

When we're making a decision with another, we need to share our feelings about the options. We may be afraid to explore all options because the other may prefer one that we don't like. Or they may not understand our preferences and we may get into an argument.

In a close relationship we will rarely be happy with a decision that didn't take all our feelings into account. We usually have a bundle of different feelings about an option, and once we express one feeling the others will come to the fore. We can share our feelings with the least risk by using "I" messages and listening to the other as if they had also used them.

Personal Affirmations

I, (your name), share my feelings with "I" messages.

You, (your name), share your feelings with "I" messages.

(Your name) shares her/his feelings with "I" messages.

We, (your name) and (other's name), share our feelings with "I" messages.

Reciprocal Affirmations

I, (your name), share my feelings with "I" messages.

You, (other's name), share your feelings with "I" messages.

We, (your name) and (other's name), share our feelings with "I" messages.

(Your name) and (other's name) share their feelings with "I" messages.

Even though we consciously try very hard, it sometimes seems difficult to change old negative behaviors. It can be frustrating to try so hard and not be completely successful immediately.

If we concentrate on the new positive behavior, rather than on consciously changing the old negative behavior, we find that the new positive behavior takes over and the old negative disappears. It takes less effort to learn and practice a new behavior than to agonize over an old one. The new, in effect, crowds out the old.

Personal Affirmations

I, (your name), crowd out negative behaviors with positive ones.

You, (your name), crowd out negative behaviors with positive ones.

(Your name) crowds out negative behaviors with positive ones.

We, (your name) and (other's name), crowd out negative behaviors with positive ones.

Reciprocal Affirmations

I, (your name), crowd out negative behaviors with positive ones.

You, (other's name), crowd out negative behaviors with positive ones.

We, (your name) and (other's name), crowd out negative behaviors with positive ones.

(Your name) and (other's name) crowd out negative behaviors with positive ones.

On a bright sunny day I usually feel on top of the world. On a rainy, low-pressure day I often feel down. I now realize that weather and high and low barometric pressure can affect my moods. I now know I don't have anyone else to blame for my moods. In fact, sharing with someone close to me that it's my problem with the weather, not with them, can help our relationship.

I now have the opportunity to make the best of the weather. We need the rain for the flowers and crops, and the moisture helps my sinuses. Personal awareness turns my mood into a happier one.

Personal Affirmations

I, (your name), turn my weather-related lows into happier times.

You, (your name), turn your weather-related lows into happier times.

(Your name) turns her/his weather-related lows into happier times.

We, (your name) and (other's name), turn our weather-related lows into happier times.

Reciprocal Affirmations

I, (your name), turn my weather-related lows into happier times.

You, (other's name), turn your weather-related lows into happier times.

We, (your name) and (other's name), turn our weather-related lows into happier times.

(Your name) and (other's name) turn their weather-related lows into happier times.

When we impart information to others, we may have very specific expectations of what they will do with it. We base our expectations on things they have said or done in the past or on desires or motives we have surmised from our past experiences with them.

When we impart information in this way, we have fertile ground for misunderstanding. If we have guessed correctly, the other may still resent our limiting their freedom to change their mind. If we are wrong, we both may proceed under false assumptions until there is some major consequence. When giving information, we need to give context by expressing our feelings, our purpose and any expectations.

Personal Affirmations

I, (your name), share my feelings and purpose when I give information.

You, (your name), share your feelings and purpose when you give information.

(Your name) shares her/his feelings and purpose when she/he gives information.

We, (your name) and (other's name), share our feelings and purpose when we give information.

Reciprocal Affirmations

I, (your name), share my feelings and purpose when I give you information.

You, (other's name), share your feelings and purpose when you give me information.

We, (your name) and (other's name), share our feelings and purpose when we give each other information.

(Your name) and (other's name) share their feelings and purpose when they give each other information.

Most of us get together with our families over the holidays. We often do this with relatives we rarely choose to see otherwise. We take the opportunity to renew and revitalize inherited relationships, to go back to our roots.

A few minutes chatting with each relative can help reestablish our connection and renew and revitalize our relationship. The holiday get-together can give us a sense of belonging that may be hard to find in any meaningful sense in our everyday life.

Personal Affirmations

I, (your name), revitalize my family relationships over the holidays.

You, (your name), revitalize your family relationships over the holidays.

(Your name) revitalizes her/his family relationships over the holidays.

We, (your name) and (other's name), revitalize our family relationships over the holidays.

Reciprocal Affirmations

I, (your name), revitalize my family relationships over the holidays.

You, (other's name), revitalize your family relationships over the holidays.

We, (your name) and (other's name), revitalize our family relationships over the holidays.

(Your name) and (other's name) revitalize their family relationships over the holidays.

No matter what we do, no matter how right it is for us, there is always someone who thinks we look foolish, stupid or wrong. If we tried to please everyone, we wouldn't do anything. Oops — somebody doesn't like us doing nothing, either!

How, then, can we avoid appearing foolish or wrong? We can't. So we needn't even try. We can stop agonizing over whether some action or inaction may make us look foolish to someone. It will. Instead we can get on with life and disregard how we may look to others. We must enjoy living in a way that is right for us.

Personal Affirmations

I, (your name), don't worry about what others may
    think of my actions.

You, (your name), don't worry about what others may
    think of your actions.

(Your name) doesn't worry about what others may
    think of her/his actions.

We, (your name) and (other's name), don't worry
    about what others may think of our actions.

Reciprocal Affirmations

I, (your name), don't worry about what you may think
    of my actions.

You, (other's name), don't worry about what I may
    think of your actions.

We, (your name) and (other's name), don't worry
    about what the other may think of our actions.

(Your name) and (other's name) don't worry about
    what the other may think of their actions.

One of our most anxiety-producing relationships, and potentially our most satisfying one, is our sexual relationship. In the popular culture intercourse is equated with a sexual relationship.

But there are many ways we can communicate sexually. Our goal is feelings of intimacy, closeness and caring. Some ways to express these feelings sexually are sharing feelings, revealing vulnerability, affectionate touching, hugging and making tender compliments, as well as intercourse. All of the means of sexual communication are important in a healthy, satisfying sex life.

Personal Affirmations

I, (your name), have lots of ways to express my sexual relationship.

You, (your name), have lots of ways to express your sexual relationship.

(Your name) has lots of ways to express her/his sexual relationship.

We, (your name) and (other's name), have lots of ways to express our sexual relationship.

Reciprocal Affirmations

I, (your name), have lots of ways to express our sexual relationship.

You, (other's name), have lots of ways to express our sexual relationship.

We, (your name) and (other's name), have lots of ways to express our sexual relationship.

(Your name) and (other's name) have lots of ways to express their sexual relationship.

When we decide to focus less on doing, accomplishing and making things happen and more on just "being," we may resist. Being seems so inactive, unfocused and self-indulgent. We remember times we've done nothing and wonder how these experiences could be helpful, such as mindlessly watching television, telling others to leave us alone when we're frustrated or exhausted, or abandoning goals of better eating or more exercising.

The state of being we must aspire to, however, is the opposite of vegetating, isolating ourselves or giving up. It's a heightened awareness of life and ourselves, a connectedness with all others at the level of mind and a clearer vision of multiple options and present delights.

Personal Affirmations
I, (your name), enjoy a vibrant state of being.
You, (your name), enjoy a vibrant state of being.
(Your name) enjoys a vibrant state of being.
We, (your name) and (other's name), enjoy vibrant states of being.

Reciprocal Affirmations
I, (your name), enjoy a vibrant state of being.
You, (other's name), enjoy a vibrant state of being.
We, (your name) and (other's name), enjoy vibrant states of being.
(Your name) and (other's name) enjoy vibrant states of being.

If we feel bored by the routine of home, work or a relationship, how can we break out? One of the ways is through play. Play is a fun time of goofing off with no goals in mind. Play renews us.

We need to take time and give ourselves permission to do something fun each day, even if only for a few minutes. We need to play by ourselves for our own benefit and play with others for the benefit of our relationship. Personal play might be casually reading a magazine or singing along with our favorite song. Play together can be a walk in the park, listening to music or dancing in the street.

Personal Affirmations

I, (your name), take time to play every day.

You, (your name), take time to play every day.

(Your name) takes time to play every day.

We, (your name) and (other's name), take time to play every day.

Reciprocal Affirmations

I, (your name), take time to play with you every day.

You, (other's name), take time to play with me every day.

We, (your name) and (other's name), take time to play together every day.

(Your name) and (other's name) take time to play together every day.

In a meaningful sexual relationship we are essentially enjoying each other. If we're concentrating on creating a certain physical or emotional effect in the other or ourselves, imposing specific goals or holding technical expectations, we are less likely to achieve real enjoyment.

It's through truly spontaneous, natural sharing that we get sexual enjoyment. Good sex is a high-energy event requiring our total absorption. We need to focus our minds on what we find in our partner to enjoy — their love for us, their body, parts of their body we especially appreciate, their latest endearing words, shared interests, dreams or memories. These things make me feel good about giving myself totally to my partner for full personal enjoyment.

Personal Affirmations

I, (your name), focus on enjoying my sexual partner.

You, (your name), focus on enjoying your sexual partner.

(Your name) focuses on enjoying her/his sexual partner.

We, (your name) and (other's name), focus on enjoying each other sexually.

Reciprocal Affirmations

I, (your name), focus on enjoying you sexually.

You, (other's name), focus on enjoying me sexually.

We, (your name) and (other's name), focus on enjoying each other sexually.

(Your name) and (other's name) focus on enjoying each other sexually.

We learn a lot about others from hearing their voice as they speak. Their emotion, from joy to desperation; their volume, from soft to screaming; and their tone, from normal to whining or sweet to sarcastic, tell us much about their current state.

By the same token, our voice tells others a lot about us. Can we expect good responses from others when we are loud, angry and whining? Or quiet, resigned and fearful? We can control the way we speak. The first step is being conscious of our voice. The second step is desiring to change it. The third step is practicing the changes.

Personal Affirmations
I, (your name), pay attention to how I speak to others.
You, (your name), pay attention to how you speak to others.
(Your name) pays attention to how she/he speaks to others.
We, (your name) and (other's name), pay attention to how we speak to others.

Reciprocal Affirmations
I, (your name), pay attention to how I speak to you.
You, (other's name), pay attention to how you speak to me.
We, (your name) and (other's name), pay attention to how we speak to each other.
(Your name) and (other's name) pay attention to how they speak to each other.

Each of us is entitled to our own personal space, not just psychologically, but physically. We are entitled to have our personal possessions stored in a safe place and secure against use or abuse by anyone who has not received our prior express permission. We are also entitled to a private place and time to use our personal effects, whether for grooming, dressing, reading, sitting, meditating, stretching, sleeping, doing nothing or whatever we want.

If we feel we're always being watched, that someone else is constantly judging whether we're doing well or using our tools or time wisely, we must acknowledge and assert our right to a personal space completely free of others' opinions or commentary.

Personal Affirmations

I, (your name), deserve a physical space for myself.

You, (your name), deserve a physical space for yourself.

(Your name) deserves a physical space for herself/himself.

We, (your name) and (other's name), each deserve a physical space of our own.

Reciprocal Affirmations

I, (your name), deserve a physical space of my own.

You, (other's name), deserve a physical space of your own.

We, (your name) and (other's name), each deserve a physical space of our own.

(Your name) and (other's name) each deserve a physical space of their own.

In sexual matters we often do for the other what we would like them most to do for us. While it sounds like the Golden Rule, it's really a substitution of example-setting for good communication. Often neither partner is happy in sex because each is doing what they would like done to them but neither is getting what they want. For example, if one likes kisses and the other hugs as signs of affection, neither will ever receive the signs they appreciate most.

Communication about sex may be as important as communication in sex. We need to ask for what we like — once we have asked ourselves what we like — and then also ask the other what they like.

Personal Affirmations

I, (your name), feel good about asking for what I want in sex.

You, (your name), feel good about asking for what you want in sex.

(Your name) feels good about asking for what she/he wants in sex.

We, (your name) and (other's name), feel good about asking each other for what we want in sex.

Reciprocal Affirmations

I, (your name), feel good about asking you for what I want in sex.

You, (other's name), feel good about asking me for what you want in sex.

We, (your name) and (other's name), feel good about asking each other for what we want in sex.

(Your name) and (other's name) feel good about asking each other for what they want in sex.

The holiday season is busy for all of us with shopping, wrapping, baking, decorating, partying and visiting friends and relatives. We often get so caught up in the whirl of activities, buying presents, doing things or going places to please others, that we have little or no time left to do the things that please us most about the holidays.

We must remember to take time throughout the holiday season to do the things that make the holidays special for us. It's important to meet our own needs during the holiday season as well as the rest of the year.

Personal Affirmations

I, (your name), find time for the holiday activities I
  enjoy most.

You, (your name), find time for the holiday activities
  you enjoy most.

(Your name) finds time for the holiday activities she/he
  enjoys most.

We, (your name) and (other's name), find time for the
  holiday activities we enjoy most.

Reciprocal Affirmations

I, (your name), find time for the holiday activities I
  enjoy most.

You, (other's name), find time for the holiday activities
  you enjoy most.

We, (your name) and (other's name), find time for the
  holiday activities we enjoy most.

(Your name) and (other's name) find time for the
  holiday activities they enjoy most.

When we step out into the world, we see all kinds of people in all kinds of costumes. People come from different economic backgrounds, have different ethnic makeup, and wear costumes from laborer to executive, store clerk to military.

At the core, we're all just people. We may be wrapped in different clothes and radiate different attitudes, but on the deepest level we all have the same fears and aspirations. Deep down we start at the same place.

Armed with this knowledge, we can relate to all kinds of people without fear.

Personal Affirmations

I, (your name), know I have something in common with everybody.

You, (your name), know you have something in common with everybody.

(Your name) knows she/he has something in common with everybody.

We, (your name) and (other's name), know we have something in common with everybody.

Reciprocal Affirmations

I, (your name), know I have something in common with everybody.

You, (other's name), know you have something in common with everybody.

We, (your name) and (other's name), know we have something in common with everybody.

(Your name) and (other's name) know they have something in common with everybody.

If those close to us seem unable to share our good feelings with us, we need not give up. We have other options for ways to express ourselves. Perhaps we have not set the stage adequately. We need to give a context to good news so others can put themselves in our place and resist reacting with jealousy, skepticism or impatience.

Perhaps we would get through to them better if we used "I" messages. This allows the other the freedom to share or not share our feelings and makes them more inclined to share. Also, we might first show an interest in what they are feeling. This attention helps put them in the mood to hear good news.

Personal Affirmations

I, (your name), prepare others for my good news.
You, (your name), prepare others for your good news.
(Your name) prepares others for her/his good news.
We, (your name) and (other's name), prepare others
*   for our good news.*

Reciprocal Affirmations

I, (your name), prepare you for my good news.
You, (other's name), prepare me for your good news.
We, (your name) and (other's name), prepare each
*   other for our good news.*
(Your name) and (other's name) prepare each other
*   for their good news.*

We've all been raised with the idea that we need to be courteous to everyone with whom we come into contact. Many of us also see our home as our castle, as a place to relax where we don't have to put on airs. As part of our relaxing, we may drop all or part of our politeness. "Please," "thank you," "I'm sorry" and "excuse me" go out the window.

Those we live with have high expectations of being treated politely because, after all, we love them much more than strangers to whom we are polite. We need to remember that politeness isn't just something for strangers. Politeness can make our daily life smoother and more enjoyable.

Personal Affirmations

I, (your name), am polite, especially to those close to me.

You, (your name), are polite, especially to those close to you.

(Your name) is polite, especially to those close to her/him.

We, (your name) and (other's name), are polite, especially to those close to us.

Reciprocal Affirmations

I, (your name), am polite, especially to you.

You, (other's name), are polite, especially to me.

We, (your name) and (other's name), are polite, especially to each other.

(Your name) and (other's name) are polite, especially to each other.

Most of my busy life is spent doing, accomplishing and achieving. One of my great pleasures is a moment, an hour, a day or a week spent just being. Not accomplishing, not achieving, not doing. Just being. Living in the moment. Living for the moment, not for the past or the future.

Relating through beingness is joyful and relaxing. It's relating without tension, stress or demands. It's enjoying the other as they are at this moment. Not as we wish them to be, but just as they are.

Personal Affirmations

I, (your name), make time for just being together.
You, (your name), make time for just being together.
(Your name) makes time for just being together.
We, (your name) and (other's name), make time for just being together.

Reciprocal Affirmations

I, (your name), make time for just being with you.
You, (other's name), make time for just being with me.
We, (your name) and (other's name), make time for just being together.
(Your name) and (other's name) make time for just being together.

An optimist expects things to get better. A pessimist expects things to get worse. A realist knows things will get worse if they don't do their part to make them better. If we fear change because we're afraid things will get worse, they probably will. Participants in long-term relationships who feel successful usually feel confident that it doesn't hurt to rock the boat.

Asking others to adjust to accommodate our needs when we develop new needs more often brings good than bad. A series of small improvements tends eventually to become a qualitative change for the better, while an unchanging relationship tends to stagnate and turn stale.

Personal Affirmations
I, (your name), do my part to make things better.
You, (your name), do your part to make things better.
(Your name) does her/his part to make things better.
We, (your name) and (other's name), do our part to make things better.

Reciprocal Affirmations
I, (your name), do my part to make things better.
You, (other's name), do your part to make things better.
We, (your name) and (other's name), do our part to make things better.
(Your name) and (other's name) do their part to make things better.

Sometimes we cling to old relationships out of fear of making new ones. We ask more and more of those close in order to avoid the risks of building new connections. We dwell on gossip about misunderstood intentions, breakups and betrayals to justify our complacency. "Better safe than sorry" echoes in our minds. But this old childhood adage has no place in mature life. ·

Each person who crosses our path has a purpose in our lives. From giving a smile at the checkout counter to introducing ourselves to a stranger at a social gathering, we need to take opportunities to increase our sources of comfort, strength and enjoyment.

Personal Affirmations

I, (your name), take the risk of connecting with new people.

You, (your name), take the risk of connecting with new people.

(Your name) takes the risk of connecting with new people.

We, (your name) and (other's name), take the risk of connecting with new people.

Reciprocal Affirmations

I, (your name), take the risk of connecting with new people.

You, (other's name), take the risk of connecting with new people.

We, (your name) and (other's name), take the risk of connecting with new people.

(Your name) and (other's name) take the risk of connecting with new people.

Feeling close to those we love is hard when we see too little of them. Often work schedules mean we don't see the other for 12 or 16 hours or even longer on a daily basis. For those who travel frequently, it could be several days before we see the other again.

Tender touching before we part, such as a lingering hug, can help us feel close. And when we're reunited, more tender touching begins the process of re-establishing our closeness. Other ingredients are gentle words and time spent renewing our common feelings after a period of different experiences.

Personal Affirmations

I, (your name), use time and touching to re-establish closeness.

You, (your name), use time and touching to re-establish closeness.

(Your name) uses time and touching to re-establish closeness.

We, (your name) and (other's name), use time and touching to re-establish closeness.

Reciprocal Affirmations

I, (your name), use time and touching to re-establish closeness with you.

You, (other's name), use time and touching to re-establish closeness with me.

We, (your name) and (other's name), use time and touching to re-establish closeness with each other.

(Your name) and (other's name) use time and touching to re-establish closeness with each other.

When we seek to expand our friendships or connect more openly with other people in our lives, it can be helpful to release any barriers we may have built up based on economic, educational, or other distinctions. As college graduates, for example, we may have come to think we have little in common with those who have only high school diplomas or less. Or as clerical or service workers we may act very deferentially toward professionals.

To release barriers and prejudgments, let's remind ourselves that all are human together, all are challenged with similar feelings and stresses, and each can help the other with unexpected insights and new enjoyments of life.

Personal Affirmations

I, (your name), release any prejudgments in making friends.

You, (your name), release any prejudgments in making friends.

(Your name) releases any prejudgments in making friends.

We, (your name) and (other's name), release any prejudgments in making friends.

Reciprocal Affirmations

I, (your name), release any prejudgments in making friends.

You, (other's name), release any prejudgments in making friends.

We, (your name) and (other's name), release any prejudgments in making friends.

(Your name) and (other's name) release any prejudgments in making friends.

It's true in our relationships as well as in everything else that the only constant is change. We all grow continually. We need to make adjustments in our relationships to reflect the changes we're experiencing and make our relationships even better.

Often the little things that bother me seem petty compared to the overall satisfaction I receive from my relationship. Yet I find it worthwhile to address those little things in a spirit of trying to make a good thing better.

Personal Affirmations

I, (your name), work on even the little things.

You, (your name), work on even the little things.

(Your name) works on even the little things.

We, (your name) and (other's name), work on even the little things.

Reciprocal Affirmations

I, (your name), work on even the little things.

You, (other's name), work on even the little things.

We, (your name) and (other's name), work together on even the little things.

(Your name) and (other's name) work together on even the little things.

No relationship stands alone. If only one person, thing or activity counts to us, the relationship will not be able to meet our needs. Life is a fantastic intricate web of relationships. Each affects others and each depends on others. Only a Supreme Power can grasp the full design.

Our job is to tend the relationships that touch us. Do we have lover or spouse, children, parents-in-law, cousins, friends or co-workers? Can we heal relations with parents, even if they're no longer with us? Do we have pets, keep plants, write Senators? Our lives touch others through our relationships. As our relationships grow, so do we.

Personal Affirmations

I, (your name), tend all my relationships.

You, (your name), tend all your relationships.

(Your name) tends all her/his relationships.

We, (your name) and (other's name), tend all our relationships.

Reciprocal Affirmations

I, (your name), tend all my relationships.

You, (other's name), tend all your relationships.

We, (your name) and (other's name), tend all our relationships.

(Your name) and (other's name) tend all their relationships.

Just as we need to take care not to blame others when we have negative feelings, we need to take care not to burden others with responsibility when we have positive feelings. No one is responsible for making or keeping someone else happy, even though often we do speak and think of "making each other happy." As a shorthand for mutual enjoyment, these words are well understood. But if we speak repeatedly as if we're depending on the other for our good feelings, the relationship will become more burden than pleasure.

When we feel good about others, we need to recognize that it's a matter of our choice, not theirs.

Personal Affirmations

I, (your name), choose to feel good about others.
You, (your name), choose to feel good about others.
(Your name) chooses to feel good about others.
We, (your name) and (other's name), choose to feel good about others.

Reciprocal Affirmations

I, (your name), choose to feel good about you.
You, (other's name), choose to feel good about me.
We, (your name) and (other's name), choose to feel good about each other.
(Your name) and (other's name) choose to feel good about each other.

It's an act of love and generosity to share the fruits of our labor with someone else. It's not merely a duty we can take for granted. Each adult has the responsibility to care for him or herself. In a relationship, we can delegate that responsibility to our partner if they agree to take it. We can share and blend our incomes or keep our finances distinct. Particular arrangements aren't right or wrong. What matters is that they are comfortable for both partners.

I will take responsibility for discussing, reviewing and adjusting my financial arrangements to accommodate our mutual needs. Our different expectations can be reconciled in love.

Personal Affirmations

I, (your name), take first responsibility for my finances.

You, (your name), take first responsibility for your finances.

(Your name) takes first responsibility for her/his finances.

We, (your name) and (other's name), each take first responsibility for our own finances.

Reciprocal Affirmations

I, (your name), take first responsibility for my finances.

You, (other's name), take first responsibility for your finances.

We, (your name) and (other's name), each take first responsibility for our own finances.

(Your name) and (other's name) each take first responsibility for their own finances.

We often hear that bad things happen in threes. There may be some merit to this if we think about it in the context of accident-proneness. When we experience an unexpected negative like a fall, a forgotten engagement, a fender-bender or a mean attack from another, we might view it as an isolated incident. "These things happen," we think. If a second happens, we tend to blame bad luck. It's not until a third that we get concerned and wonder how we may have helped bring on the accidents.

Accident-proneness occurs most often when we are overextended, tired, unfocused and feeling unloved. To make good luck we must love and take good care of ourselves.

Personal Affirmations

I, (your name), avoid accidents by taking care of myself.

You, (your name), avoid accidents by taking care of yourself.

(Your name) avoids accidents by taking care of herself/himself.

We, (your name) and (other's name), avoid accidents by taking care of ourselves.

Reciprocal Affirmations

I, (your name), avoid accidents by taking care of myself.

You, (other's name), avoid accidents by taking care of yourself.

We, (your name) and (other's name), avoid accidents by taking care of ourselves.

(Your name) and (other's name) avoid accidents by taking care of themselves.

In this holiday season we may feel overwhelmed with multiple tasks. There are decorations, food, parties, gifts, greetings, sitters, cars that don't work in the cold and extra work to help pay for it all.

It's easy to lose touch with the essence of the holiday, but we can recapture that essence. We need to take a few moments each day with our friend or lover to focus on things that make us grateful, on special moments we've had through the year or on the positive feelings we want to cultivate for the holidays. The holiday stresses then shrink quickly down to size.

Personal Affirmations

I, (your name), take a moment to nurture good holiday feelings.

You, (your name), take a moment to nurture good holiday feelings.

(Your name) takes a moment to nurture good holiday feelings.

We, (your name) and (other's name), take a moment to nurture good holiday feelings.

Reciprocal Affirmations

I, (your name), take a moment with you to nurture good holiday feelings.

You, (other's name), take a moment with me to nurture good holiday feelings.

We, (your name) and (other's name), take a moment together to nurture good holiday feelings.

(Your name) and (other's name) take a moment together to nurture good holiday feelings.

When another is bouncing off the walls with joy, how do we share it with them? We're not likely to start bouncing with them. After all, it's their feeling, not ours. Still, we want to share the feeling because we want to have some of that good feeling and we want to support the other.

As with negative feelings, we start with empathy. "I see you really feel great about that." Empathy affirms the feeling for the other, letting them know we understand. The sharing makes us feel great, too. Perhaps we'll jump up and down with them after all.

Personal Affirmations

I, (your name), use empathy to respond to positive feelings.

You, (your name), use empathy to respond to positive feelings.

(Your name) uses empathy to respond to positive feelings.

We, (your name) and (other's name), use empathy to respond to positive feelings.

Reciprocal Affirmations

I, (your name), use empathy to respond to your positive feelings.

You, (other's name), use empathy to respond to my positive feelings.

We, (your name) and (other's name), use empathy to respond to each other's positive feelings.

(Your name) and (other's name) use empathy to respond to each other's positive feelings.

Sometimes in our closest relationships we get caught in a rut of discussing only mundane subjects. Time pressures make it seem like enough just to communicate effectively about family schedules, decisions, projects and progress in school or job. But our relationship can be much enriched by finding a few minutes here and there to put these things on hold and discuss matters in the larger world beyond our household, neighborhood or office. This helps put our relationship in the context of the larger society and the world.

Even if we don't see eye-to-eye on every current event, political election, environmental issue or popular debate, we're reminded that we share the same issues and are in it together.

Personal Affirmations

I, (your name), enrich my relationships by sharing my views.

You, (your name), enrich your relationships by sharing your views.

(Your name) enriches her/his relationships by sharing her/his views.

We, (your name) and (other's name), enrich our relationships by sharing our views.

Reciprocal Affirmations

I, (your name), enrich our relationship by sharing my views.

You, (other's name), enrich our relationship by sharing your views.

We, (your name) and (other's name), enrich our relationship by sharing our views.

(Your name) and (other's name) enrich their relationship by sharing their views.

When we've decided on a course of action to improve a relationship, we sometimes get impatient and lose our momentum. When this happens, we need to ask why.

Have we nurtured a belief that things can get better, or has a little voice said we're lucky to have it so good and we don't deserve any better? Have we made a commitment to change, or have we held back a little to watch and test for results before we commit ourselves? Have we accepted the need to free up some time and energy, or have we made this into just one more chore? If we want change, we must participate actively in it.

Personal Affirmations

I, (your name), participate actively in change.

You, (your name), participate actively in change.

(Your name) participates actively in change.

We, (your name) and (other's name), participate actively in change.

Reciprocal Affirmations

I, (your name), participate actively in change.

You, (other's name), participate actively in change.

We, (your name) and (other's name), participate actively in change.

(Your name) and (other's name) participate actively in change.

Sometimes we dread family gatherings, especially of other people's families. We may feel oppressed by the multiple expectations of others who can affect our lives. Or we are eager to please but don't know everyone well enough in their present circumstances to know what they want. Or we fear prying questions when we aren't comfortable with the answers we might have to give about our job, vacation plans, progress of the children or the state of our own family.

These events will be easier if we remember that everyone else feels the same. They hope we will stick to small talk, won't launch any embarrassing quips, don't have high expectations and aren't hard to please.

Personal Affirmations

I, (your name), am easy to please at family gatherings.

You, (your name), are easy to please at family gatherings.

(Your name) is easy to please at family gatherings.

We, (your name) and (other's name), are easy to please at family gatherings.

Reciprocal Affirmations

I, (your name), am easy to please at family gatherings.

You, (other's name), are easy to please at family gatherings.

We, (your name) and (other's name), are easy to please at family gatherings.

(Your name) and (other's name) are easy to please at family gatherings.

If a positive attitude seems hard to come by, we may have to look deeper. We need a basic belief that life is good, that things can and will get better and that we can enjoy ourselves. These basic beliefs are like a well we can return to whenever we need to refresh our parched attitude and turn it positive again.

When we think about beautiful sunrises and sunsets, walks down a country lane, a baby happily playing with a rattle, and laughter with friends, it's easier to have a basic faith that life is good and we are all meant to enjoy it.

Personal Affirmations
I, (your name), have faith in the goodness of life.
You, (your name), have faith in the goodness of life.
(Your name) has faith in the goodness of life.
We, (your name) and (other's name), have faith in the goodness of life.

Reciprocal Affirmations
I, (your name), have faith in the goodness of life.
You, (other's name), have faith in the goodness of life.
We, (your name) and (other's name), have faith in the goodness of life.
(Your name) and (other's name) have faith in the goodness of life.

The special feelings of romantic love need not re-move us from reality. We need not see our loved one as perfect, the whole world, a savior or deserving of all our attention all the time. When we want to be with someone, touch them, smile at them, give them little gifts and favors, listen attentively and praise their good points, we are enriched.

It's no disadvantage that our lover isn't perfect, doesn't return every favor and cannot be the center of our universe. Romantic feelings come from within us and not from our loved one.

Personal Affirmations

I, (your name), enjoy romantic love without expecting perfection.

You, (your name), enjoy romantic love without expecting perfection.

(Your name) enjoys romantic love without expecting perfection.

We, (your name) and (other's name), enjoy romantic love without expecting perfection.

Reciprocal Affirmations

I, (your name), enjoy our romantic love without expecting perfection.

You, (other's name), enjoy our romantic love without expecting perfection.

We, (your name) and (other's name), enjoy our romantic love without expecting perfection.

(Your name) and (other's name) enjoy their romantic love without expecting perfection.

When we're at a holiday gathering of extended family we can avoid uneasiness by not asking too much of ourselves or others. It's not our job to see that all goes smoothly, every joke gets a laugh, everyone enjoys our company or there are no empty silences.

The old tradition of paying one's respects can be useful at these times. Our behavior is the only matter with which we need be concerned. We might set out to have a little chat with each person and take care to harbor no specific expectations about the content. We need only create rapport for a moment to affirm our mutual acceptance within the family. We don't want to be superficial, but we do want to maintain a positive tone.

Personal Affirmations

I, (your name), chat easily with each member of the family.

You, (your name), chat easily with each member of the family.

(Your name) chats easily with each member of the family.

We, (your name) and (other's name), chat easily with each member of the family.

Reciprocal Affirmations

I, (your name), chat easily with each member of the family.

You, (other's name), chat easily with each member of the family.

We, (your name) and (other's name), chat easily with each member of the family.

(Your name) and (other's name) chat easily with each member of the family.

The greatest compliment we can give another is to tell them how much we enjoy them. "I love looking at you," is more pleasing than, "You look good, babe." The second is judgmental and may only confirm a fact they already know. In any event, the other doesn't want our judgment.

The romantics of old knew how to reach the hearts of others. They regularly told their lover how great they felt touching, smelling, looking at or even just thinking about or imagining their lover. They knew that telling their lover how they felt was the greatest compliment.

Personal Affirmations

I, (your name), tell my love how I feel about her/him.

You, (your name), tell your love how you feel about her/him.

(Your name) tells her/his love how she/he feels about her/him.

We, (your name) and (other's name), each tell the other how we feel about them.

Reciprocal Affirmations

I, (your name), tell you how I feel about you.

You, (other's name), tell me how you feel about me.

We, (your name) and (other's name), each tell the other how we feel about them.

(Your name) and (other's name) each tell the other how they feel about the other.

We can often take hints from our pets about simple, loving behavior. Our pets don't hassle, criticize or judge us. They trust us to give them what they need. As long as we fulfill some very minimal expectations, they are full of acceptance.

Sometimes, though, we have anxious pets. Perhaps they are highly inbred or they respond to a threateningly high level of tension in the home. We can learn from this how deeply anxiety can affect life, even in a being having very little comprehension of the complexities we usually blame for our anxieties.

Let's take a hint from our pets and cultivate an easy-going, guilt-free attitude.

Personal Affirmations

I, (your name), am easy-going with others.
You, (your name), are easy-going with others.
(Your name) is easy-going with others.
We, (your name) and (other's name), are easy-going with others.

Reciprocal Affirmations

I, (your name), am easy-going with you.
You, (other's name), are easy-going with me.
We, (your name) and (other's name), are easy-going with each other.
(Your name) and (other's name) are easy-going with each other.

How we say things is as important as what we say. We know this intuitively, often changing our tone, facial expression or body language to have a certain effect. If we find ourselves in a conflict, we may deny using a provocative tone or expression and claim only our words matter. But we know that our manner of speaking has an effect.

Focusing on the literal substance of our communications and ignoring how we express them leads us into more trouble as we demand ever more perfect words and send ever more conflicting messages. Instead, we need to lighten up on the exactitude of our words and tend to the tone and expression we use when we talk.

Personal Affirmations

I, (your name), speak with both tolerance and caring.

You, (your name), speak with both tolerance and caring.

(Your name) speaks with both tolerance and caring.

We, (your name) and (other's name), speak with both tolerance and caring.

Reciprocal Affirmations

I, (your name), speak to you with both tolerance and caring.

You, (other's name), speak to me with both tolerance and caring.

We, (your name) and (other's name), speak to each other with both tolerance and caring.

(Your name) and (other's name) speak to each other with both tolerance and caring.

Sometimes we pile extra work on ourselves or find ourselves in the midst of a project that requires lots of extra effort. We get fatigued and feel we're neglecting other important areas of our lives. What can we do?

First, we need a priority check. Is this extra work or project in line with our overall priorities and long-range goals? If not, we can stop. Second, we need to realize and accept that this extra burden is only temporary. If the burden is in line with our priorities and is temporary, we can do anything for a limited time.

Personal Affirmations

I, (your name), can take on an extra burden for a limited time.

You, (your name), can take on an extra burden for a limited time.

(Your name) can take on an extra burden for a limited time.

We, (your name) and (other's name), can each take on an extra burden for a limited time.

Reciprocal Affirmations

I, (your name), can take on an extra burden for a limited time.

You, (other's name), can take on an extra burden for a limited time.

We, (your name) and (other's name), can each take on an extra burden for a limited time.

(Your name) and (other's name) can each take on an extra burden for a limited time.

With so much to do and so many concerns filling our lives, we often put off rest, recreation and sleep in order to accomplish one more thing or contemplate one more problem.

Tasks get completed and problems get solved when our heads are clear and our mind and body are working efficiently. This means we must view rest and sleep as important tools in handling the rest of our lives.

But sleep and rest are valuable in themselves, too. They build our health for tomorrow and make us more agreeable and more attractive to ourselves and others. We all need adequate sleep. Let's make it a priority and put aside our cares at day's end.

Personal Affirmations

I, (your name), give myself the sleep I need.

You, (your name), give yourself the sleep you need.

(Your name) gives herself/himself the sleep she/he needs.

We, (your name) and (other's name), give ourselves the sleep we need.

Reciprocal Affirmations

I, (your name), give myself the sleep I need.

You, (other's name), give yourself the sleep you need.

We, (your name) and (other's name), give ourselves the sleep we need.

(Your name) and (other's name) give themselves the sleep they need.

How do we spend our time each day, each week, each month? Does it reflect our priorities? Would we like to spend it differently? Perhaps we have never thought about the possibilities of spending our time differently.

When we've thought about our priorities and how we would like to spend our time, it's easier to spend it in more satisfying ways. We have a choice in everything we do. Let's be proud of our positive change this year.

Personal Affirmations

I, (your name), feel good about my progress.

You, (your name), feel good about your progress.

(Your name) feels good abut her/his progress.

We, (your name) and (other's name), feel good about our progress.

Reciprocal Affirmations

I, (your name), feel good about my progress.

You, (other's name), feel good about your progress.

We, (your name) and (other's name), feel good about our progress.

(Your name) and (other's name) feel good about their progress.

Index

Abundance 242, 314

Acceptance 42, 55, 62, 237, 275, 362

Accident-proneness 352

Accidents 179, 210

Accommodate 255

Accomplishments 293

Accusations 94, 257

Achieving 343

Adjustment 165

Advice 65, 91, 126, 138, 220, 322

Advice shoppers 220

Affirm 200

Affirmations 40, 71, 143

Aging 95, 110

Agree to disagree 62

Alone 69, 140, 246, 349

Analytical 34

Anew 1

Anger 27, 47, 54, 76, 127, 257, 258, 265, 283, 303, 311, 321

Anniversaries 247

Anxiety 168, 325

Appearance 23

Appreciation 36, 141, 181

Arguments 245

Ashamed 76, 272

Asking 14, 196

Attention 5, 66, 188, 250, 259

Attitude 103, 121

Attractiveness 241, 318

Awareness 153

Balance 234, 299

Beauty 23

Begin 1

Being 153, 156, 333, 343

Belief 220, 356

Believing in people 280

Betrayed 98

Birthday 110, 293

Blame 36, 82, 258, 283, 350

Bliss 105, 288

Body 119, 134

Body language 174

Bored 334

Boundaries 167

Buddy 60, 117

Burdening 228
Burnout 206

Caring 320
Celebration 63, 114, 247
Challenges 15, 52, 197
Change 3, 16, 24, 28, 195, 234, 275, 348
Change another 108
Cheerfully 103
Child 49
Choice 96
Chores 99, 100, 282
Closeness 188, 315, 346
Comfort zone 92
Comfortable 130, 144, 168, 195, 224, 234
Commitment 7, 10, 19, 48, 190, 201, 230, 279, 356
Common dreams 298
Common experiences 308
Common philosophy 158
Common sense 281
Communication 19, 136, 139, 164, 168, 201, 286, 338, 355
Compassion 216
Competition 241
Competitiveness 60
Complacency 345
Complainers 289
Complaints 102, 137, 280
Complementarity 299
Compliment 361

Concerned 296
Conduct 151
Confidence 74, 173
Conflict 209
Conflicted feelings 205
Confrontation 112, 193
Connection 246, 304, 309, 319
Conscious awareness 69, 211
Conscious choice 123
Consciously 96, 327
Consciously change 248
Context 329
Control 70, 172, 222, 254, 303
Cooperation 99, 104, 287
Costumes 340
Courage 30, 44, 122, 163
Courtesy 159, 317, 342
Criticism 102, 171, 280
Crowd out 143, 327
Curiosity 223
Cursing 283

Darkness 268
Day-to-day 75
Death 228
Decisions 13, 65, 91, 178, 287
Defensive 171, 257, 321
Demanding 305
Denial 264

Dependence 107, 184, 238, 241
Depression 51, 233, 297
Deserve 85
Desires 263
Despair 149
Desperation 160
Differences 124, 207, 256, 299, 340
Disagreement 9, 163
Discouraged 297
Disease 233
Dreams 31, 68, 115, 252
Dressing 226

Empathy 52, 109, 131, 177, 251, 253, 354
Endorphins 302
Energy 48, 180, 201
Enjoyment 182, 223, 316, 324, 335
Enthusiasm 114, 224
Equality 287, 309
Equilibrium 172
Escalating 192
Exaggerations 43
Example 291
Exciting 75
Exercise 67, 76
Exhaustion 233
Expectations 6, 31, 39, 295, 303, 329, 357
Experience 227
Experiment 190

Explanations 167, 264
Expression 363
Eye contact 139, 323

Failure 2, 70
Faith 358
Faith in people 98
Family 78, 330
Family gatherings 357, 360
Fantastic web 349
Fatigued 364
Fear 30, 83, 113
Feel stuck 96
Feeling close 152
Feeling vocabulary 120
Feelings 123, 166, 170, 199, 218, 232, 326
Financial 168, 238, 273, 351
Find solutions 40
Flexibility 33, 185, 282
Flirting 279
Food 318
Foolish 64, 296, 331
Force 276, 319
Forgetfulness 210
Forgiveness 127, 260
Freedom 8, 146, 184, 290
Friction 207, 256
Friends 150, 197, 243, 285, 300, 347
Friendship 15, 129, 241
Frustrated 322, 333
Fun 147, 223, 249, 316

369

Generation 313
Generosity 239, 314
Giving 269
Goals 2, 180, 184
Good companion 186
Good feelings 151
Good judgment 216
Good news 140, 286, 341
Good points 318
Good qualities 87
Goodness 358
Greeting 250, 317
Growth 84
Guess our feelings 50
Guilt 65, 83, 88, 170

Habits 143, 211, 248
Happiness 121, 214, 231, 304, 350
Happy emotions 292
Heal ourselves 253
Health 35, 126, 233, 235, 310
Hear 321
Help 297
Helpful suggestions 94
Helplessness 242
Holiday 330, 339, 353, 360
Home 237
Honesty 167, 219
Hope 115, 149, 276
Hug 21, 130, 338
Humor 57, 106, 142, 307

"I" messages 166, 326, 341
Imaginary 312
Immediate gratification 316
Impatience 221
Important 236
Independence 125, 186, 196
Individuality 184
Influence 319
Information 329
Inner child 47
Inner explorations 161
Inner knowledge 138
Insistence 264
Internal timing 270
Interrupting 66, 159
Intimacy 5, 158, 294, 301
Isolation 149

Jealousy 107, 290
Job 78, 172
Joint decisions 25, 81, 209
Joint goals 213
Joy 132, 147, 150
Judgment 26, 34, 113, 146, 216

Kindness 135, 267, 305, 320
Kisses 21, 130, 338

Labels 94
Laughing 217

Learn 271
Lessons 271
Let go 4, 156, 213
Levels 43
Lifestyle 173
Light 268
Lighter side 296
Listening 11, 189, 205, 212, 252, 300
Living this moment 41
Living today 95
Long-term relationships 169, 306
Look for the good 106
Looking foolish 113
Loss 187
Love 21, 53, 55, 85, 161, 236, 263, 269

Manageable 267
Manipulation 73, 104, 230
Mediocrity 64
Meeting new people 124, 162
Mentor 22, 204
Mind 119
Mind and body 231, 365
Mistakes 190, 272
Misunderstandings 164
Model 291
Moment 343
Money 56, 61, 273
Moods 102, 116, 259, 328
Motives 100

Multiple feelings 169, 170
Music 171, 175
Mutual decisions 193
Mutual support 19, 201

Nagging 126, 310
Name 323
Nature 80, 101, 284
Necessities 236
Needs 4, 29, 72, 186, 235, 263, 314, 344
Negative behaviors 327
Negative thinking 94, 143
Negativity 268
Network 349
New experiences 224
New people 124, 162, 345
New responses 1
Nuclear family 243
Nurturing 108

Obligation 187
Older people 243, 278, 313
Opportunity 200, 261
Opposites 299
Optimism 288, 344
Options 109, 220, 326
Others' ideas 189
Outlook on life 103
Overrationalize 266
Overwhelmed 353
Overwhelming 274

Pain 46, 77, 228, 253

Parenting 49
Passive 195
Past 183, 214
Past patterns 1
Patience 39, 86, 276, 319
Patterns 32, 122, 175
Payoff 239
Peace 55, 172, 237, 284
Perception 144
Perfect mate 230
Perfection 6, 87, 285, 300, 359
Permission 337
Persistence 24
Personal hygiene 74
Personal space 337
Personal style 44, 207
Perspective 274, 284
Pessimism 93, 288, 344
Pets 157, 362
Physical 134
Physical intimacy 203
Plans 3, 185
Plateau 234
Play 90, 146, 334
Pleading 264
Please everyone 331
Pleasing 206
Pleasure 114, 132, 147
Politeness 342
Positive 307
Positive attitude 93, 119, 277, 358

Positive feelings 120, 136, 350
Positive mood 119
Power 28
Power to change 183
Praise 206
Predictability 92
Preferences 219
Prejudgments 347
Preoccupation 191, 210
Present 83, 288
Priorities 29, 366
Priority check 364
Privacy 294
Private agenda 213
Problem solving 220
Problems 82, 133
Productiveness 176
Progress 86, 355
Projecting 265
Proposer and disposer 26
Prosperity 59
Provocative tone 363
Put-downs 43, 225

Rapport 319
Rational powers 266
Realist 344
Receiving 269
Reciprocate 135
Rejection 149
Relationship with myself 20, 79

Relationship with
   ourselves 20, 244
Release 217
Renewal 63, 80, 198
Resentment 36, 112, 235
Respect 133
Respectful 267
Responsibility 17, 50, 69,
   137, 230, 254
Rest 365
Reward 36, 63
Right to be left alone 167
Right way 193
Risk 16
Roles 204
Romantic love 45, 359
Romantics 361
Routine 33, 165, 215, 334

Sacrifice 314
Same sex 241
Sarcasm 225
Satisfaction 145, 176, 348
Scarcity 242, 314
Schedules 355
Second chance 88
Second-guessing 8, 167,
   212
Self-criticism 134
Self-esteem 22, 194, 226,
   251, 262, 295
Self-image 241
Self-pity 46
Selfishness 53

Sensory perceptions 298
Separate experiences 309
Separate interests 125
Sex 128, 148, 152, 155,
   203, 219, 312, 335, 338
Sexual 301, 332
Sexual communication 227
Sexual intimacy 58
Sexual response 37
Sexual satisfaction 240
Sexuality 202
Shame 311
Sharing 99, 101, 124, 232,
   242, 292
Silence 167
Silliness 64, 90
Skepticism 286
Skills 145, 180
Sleep 179, 365
Small things 249
Smiles 51, 231, 277
Solutions 52, 82, 251
Sorry 342
Space 42, 91, 229
Special gifts 141
Spending 56, 61
Spontaneity 223, 240, 335
Spring 80
Strangers 162, 277, 315
Strength 253
Stress 67, 72, 77, 128, 182
Strings 269
Struggle 119
Student 22, 204

Stupid 64, 331
Style 226
Subconscious 212
Sunset law 33
Sympathy 131

Taking stock 293
Tension 10, 217, 264
Thirst 233
Time 89, 154, 176, 261,
    270, 325, 364, 366
Time for myself 12, 194
Together 308
Tone 265, 304, 363
Touching 21, 332, 346
Trust 97, 117, 154, 178,
    281, 320

Unappreciated 218
Unattractive 318
Uncaring 191
Unconditional 252
Unconditional love 34, 85,
    157, 216
Understanding 55, 62, 120
Undeserving 214
Union 301
Uniqueness 42
Upsets 192
Urgency 95, 178, 264, 278

Vacation 17, 198
Validate 131, 177, 309
Value 79, 145

Value system 111
Values 38
Views 355
Vision 68, 255
Vocabulary of feelings 265
Voice 18, 171, 336

Walk away 245
Wants 14, 37, 50, 61, 216,
    314
Weather 116, 328
Whole 175, 206, 262
Withdraw 167
Wonder 284
Words 43, 225, 265
Work 27, 78, 262
Worry 9, 40, 83, 88, 222
Worth 34

Yelling 283
Younger people 129, 313

Other Books By Randy Rolfe

You Can Postpone Anything But Love
Adult Children Raising Children

About The Authors

Randy Rolfe is founder of the Institute for Creative Solutions and has been a trainer and consultant on family life and preventive health for over 12 years. Formerly a practicing lawyer, she is the author of the nationally acclaimed book on spiritual parenting *You Can Postpone Anything But Love* and most recently *Adult Children Raising Children* for parents in recovery.

Jay Rolfe is an accomplished lawyer in private practice and a screenwriter.

Through a student courtship, rural homesteading, urban professional life and now family-center enterprises. Randy and Jay Rolfe have lead a rich life together built on love and communication. They share their lives with their two children in Chester County, Pennsylvania.